ON DADDY'S SHOULDERS

TOMMY TENNEY
AMIE DOCKERY

Regal

From Gospel Light
Ventura, California, U.S.A.

PUBLISHED BY REGAL BOOKS
FROM GOSPEL LIGHT
VENTURA, CALIFORNIA, U.S.A.
PRINTED IN THE U.S.A.

Regal

Regal Books is a ministry of Gospel Light, an evangelical Christian publisher dedicated to serving the local church. We believe God's vision for Gospel Light is to provide church leaders with biblical, user-friendly materials that will help them evangelize, disciple and minister to children, youth and families.

It is our prayer that this Regal book will help you discover biblical truth for your own life and help you meet the needs of others. May God richly bless you.

For a free catalog of resources from Regal Books/Gospel Light, please call your Christian supplier or contact us at 1-800-4-GOSPEL *or* www.regalbooks.com.

Cover and interior design by Robert Williams
Edited by Larry Walker

LIBRARY OF CONGRESS CATALOGING-IN-PUBLICATION DATA
Tenney, Tommy, 1956–
    On daddy's shoulders / Tommy Tenney and Amie Hayes-Dockery.
        p. cm.
    ISBN 0-8307-2793-0
  1. Parenting—Religious aspects—Christianity. 2. Christian children—Religious life. I. Hayes-Dockery, Amie. II. Title.
    BV4529.T47 2003
    248.8'45—dc21   2003000224

1 2 3 4 5 6 7 8 9 10 11 12 13 14 15 / 09 08 07 06 05 04 03

Rights for publishing this book in other languages are contracted by Gospel Light Worldwide, the international nonprofit ministry of Gospel Light. Gospel Light Worldwide also provides publishing and technical assistance to international publishers dedicated to producing Sunday School and Vacation Bible School curricula and books in the languages of the world. For additional information, visit www.gospellightworldwide.org; write to Gospel Light Worldwide, P.O. Box 3875, Ventura, CA 93006; or send an e-mail to info@gospellightworldwide.org.

DEDICATION

If you sit on someone's shoulders, the law of perspective dictates how far you see. Those who are upon the shoulders of giants see further.

My "understanding" is three generations deep. Under me stand giants: parents and grandparents whose words and lives lifted me so that I could see further. It is to these godly giants in the land that I dedicate this labor of love.

Even a "midget" like me should be able to "see" from the vantage point where I have been privileged to sit.

TOMMY TENNEY

To my parents, who not only put me on their shoulders but also asked me "What do you see?"

AMIE DOCKERY

CONTENTS

INTRODUCTION

If it is your habit to skip introductions because they seem boring or irrelevant, I urge you to make an exception this time. Most introductions introduce a book, but I want to introduce a person and tell you about a relationship that produced the book you're holding in your hand.

I didn't coauthor this book with Amie Dockery because I needed another book to write. I worked with Amie because I believe in her, her family and her calling, and also because of the weight of our shared history.

Amie is young enough to be one of my daughters, and in fact, she is the daughter of one of my longtime friends, Mike Hayes. This book is a product of generational linkage from family to family and generation to generation. Amie tapped a deep generational well of godly faithfulness, and she labored with me to offer you a life-giving drink from the well of wisdom. This book contains one of the important biblical keys you need in order to pass along or *receive* a true inheritance from one generation to the next. The only way you will know is if you take a drink.

TOMMY TENNEY

———————————

Some time ago my parents asked me to accompany them to a Christian booksellers convention where they would meet with several publishers to discuss my father's book project. I was excited about the opportunity and wondered what would become of the manuscript I had helped him write.

My father often asked me to sit in on such meetings, but I clearly remember this meeting in particular. Every chair in the meeting area was occupied, so I quietly took a seat on the floor. When I noticed that all of the men in the room seemed uncomfortable with the arrangement, I told them, "I am not here to be seen or heard; I'm only here to listen."

I was thrilled simply to be there, and I can still remember the rush of gratitude I felt for the opportunity to attend that meeting. I didn't realize that I was about to take a sneak peak at an unexpected possibility for my life.

Although I dreamed of one day authoring my own books, the prospect seemed absolutely out of reach at the time. The truth is that it *would* have been out of reach had I not entered that meeting courtesy of "my daddy's shoulders."

It was during that meeting where I sat on the floor that my father mentioned my simple idea for *this* book. Within just a few months, I was writing for this project.

How did something that seemed so out of reach come to pass? My father and mother used their lives, names, influence, passion and relationships to lift my eyes and raise my reach. While they have always been faithful with what they have had to carry, they consistently treated me more like a gift than a burden.

The difference between gifts and burdens is the joy with which we carry them. If you know that what you are carrying is meant to bless you, you will not mind the weight or the journey.

My parents definitely did their part, but I cannot give them all of the credit. I must give God the glory He deserves. The joy I've experienced together with my parents is a shared success based on God's Word.

We can overcome the personal fears linked to the task of bringing generations together by trusting and applying the Word of God. For instance, my scriptural mission statement with regard to serving my parents has always been, "Whoever finds his life will lose it, and whoever loses his life for my sake will find it" (Matt. 10:39, *NIV*).

This highlights one of my first fears about submission. Early on I felt I would lose my own identity if I didn't venture out and do my own thing. Despite my fears, I made the commitment to work faithfully with my parents. I soon realized that I was experiencing more pleasure just being obedient to God than I had while carving away at my dream for the future.

Working with my parents has been the most rewarding experience of my life. "Thank you" just means more coming from them. I know that in the years to come the benefits will continue to grow as we build on what we have together. One piece at a time, our family message will emerge until, one day, my four children will add their vision to it.

Through this simple process of losing myself, I have found a life beyond my dreams.

First came the commitment to my parents and their ministry. After I was faithful with that, God opened other doors I didn't know were there. I am grateful for the God-given opportunities I've received, but I'm even more grateful for the relationships that give them reason.

My friendship with Tommy Tenney is one of those relationships. Through this relationship I have learned more lessons than I can put into words. We have so many things in common and yet very different perspectives. The differences in our lifestyles, ages, gender and destiny have reinforced my belief that biblical principles apply in every situation. The cross-pollination that has taken place between these pages is the story we have written together as he mentored me through this project.

In combining my perspective with Tommy's, my prayer is that your view of uniting the generations is a balanced one. By demonstrating the power of combined destiny, I hope you are encouraged to do the same.

AMIE DOCKERY

CHAPTER 1

ON DADDY'S
SHOULDERS

Nearly every parent can fill an evening with stories of the "human jungle-gym" season when children are at the climbing stage, somewhere between the ages of three and seven. If there isn't a logical reason to climb up the daddy or mommy tree, children will invent a reason.

Some weary parents may celebrate the day they ceased to be their children's favorite climbing toy, but the truth is that we are ordained to be platforms and elevators for our children all of our lives.

One of the most important and overlooked passages in the Old Testament is tucked away in a biblical "corner" just before the far more spectacular story of God's judgment over Sodom and Gomorrah.

God said of Abraham, "For I know him, that he will command his children and his household after him, and they shall keep the way of the LORD, to do justice and judgment; that the LORD may bring upon Abraham that which he hath spoken of him."[1]

Success involves *more* than the conveyance of title and authority from father to son or from mother to daughter. Destiny is more than just good training and education in the things of God, although that is a good place to start.

AMIE DOCKERY

My dad, like so many other faithful pastors past and present, had his share of holding other people's children in his arms. Yet I knew that the space on his broad shoulders was reserved for only me.

My daddy's shoulders represented a place of total acceptance and complete security for me. I took great joy in every invitation my father gave me to be drawn up high into his world.

Sometimes he galloped while I giggled uncontrollably. At other times I covered his eyes and he pretended to trip and run into things as I laughed and exulted in my "power" to trigger such playful antics.

I loved being on my daddy's shoulders. In fact, I don't remember ever asking to come down. The loftiness of my position changed my perspective of my surroundings. I felt that I could see for miles, and I thoroughly enjoyed having to duck under doors.

Every problem that looked so large to me was suddenly reduced to nothing the moment Daddy lifted me to his shoulders. In one swift movement, my father could scoop me up from the place where I was being tripped over and ignored.

He had a father's gift for making himself into a platform of power to restore my confidence, calm my fears and transform the way I viewed my world. (He still possesses that power, although I am now a grown woman with a godly husband and children of my own.)

The fulfillment of God's purposes in our families and churches demands nothing less than the successful impartation of anointing and passion for God's presence and principles from one generation to the next.

You may not have any childhood memories of times spent on your daddy's shoulders. Your earthly father may have been absent or even abusive, but your heavenly Father said He would be a "father to the fatherless."[2] The scriptural principle of adoption allows you even to adopt childhood stories of others as your own.

Destiny is more than just good training and education in the things of God, although that is a good place to start.

Allow the scenes described in the Bible to form a powerful picture and reveal the spiritual significance of what it means to ride on the heavenly Father's shoulders. This is a portrait of the purpose and plan of God for every generation.

Without that picture, it may be difficult to harness the power and personally become a platform to help your descendants ascend to their God-ordained destiny.

TURN THE TIDE OF DESTINY WITH ONE LIFE

As far as the spirit realm is concerned, your "loving lift" literally empowers your children to start out in life as millionaires! It gives them a leg up on the world with a real advantage and opportunity to make a greater difference in the world. You have an obligation to teach your children and those you've "adopted" that it is possible to turn the tide of destiny with one life—their own.

The modern nation of Israel would not be the same today if it were not for the destiny and determination of a Lithuanian Jew named Eliezer Perlman. In 1880, he launched himself into the impossible task of reviving the Hebrew language, even though it had been dead for many centuries!

He changed his name to Eliezer Ben Yehuda (son of Judah) and immigrated to Palestine (Israel as a nation would not be reborn for 67 years). He and his new bride decided to set up a Hebrew-speaking home just to prove to other Jews that it could be done.

On a Quest to Reclaim the Ancient Biblical Language

Eliezer Ben Yehuda edited a number of Hebrew-language newspapers and used them to introduce freshly translated Hebrew words and to coin new modern words to update the ancient language. Despite tremendous persecution, even from other Jews and especially from enemies of the Zionist cause, Ben Yehuda continued to conduct research and scour the libraries of Europe in a quest to reclaim the ancient biblical language of his people word by word.

He had an odd habit of writing tidbits of research on tiny pieces of paper and "filing" them with thousands of others in a cluttered office. Yet in the end, he always seemed to know where they were. How gratifying it must have been to finally have the pleasure of hearing Hebrew spoken by people in the streets of Palestine's cities.

Author Lance Lambert wrote in his book *The Uniqueness of Israel* that "by 1916, 40 percent of the Jewish population in Palestine spoke Hebrew as their first language."[3] Hebrew was declared to be the national language of Israel when that nation was reborn in 1948, and to this day Hebrew scholars continue to carry on Ben Yehuda's work.

"That [Hebrew] is today a language used for everything from football to nuclear physics is owed largely, under God, to one man, Eliezer Ben Yehuda," Lambert writes. "I say 'under God' for, in my opinion, there is no adequate explanation for the miracle of the rebirth of Hebrew other than that God was behind it."[4]

Isaiah prophesied about the coming Messiah with these words: "And He has made My mouth like a sharp sword; in the shadow of His hand He has hidden Me, and made Me a polished shaft; in His quiver He has hidden Me."[5]

You and your children are also "polished," or select, arrows in the quiver of God. He fully intends to shoot you into the future toward the mark of your divine destiny and purpose.

TOMMY TENNEY

After my dad tore the rotator cuff in his shoulder, he underwent reconstructive surgery. For a while, no grandchildren could be perched on that shoulder. It had to be restored before it could once again lift others higher.

Eliezer Ben Yehuda accepted the task of reconstructing Hebrew, the ancient language of the Bible. This heritage had been torn from the lives of the Jews, but once it was restored, it became a great "shoulder" that helped lift and shape the identity of the modern nation of Israel. Ironically, that nation was "born in a day" in fulfillment of Bible prophecy (see Isaiah 66:8) passed on to us in the Hebrew language.

Polishing perfects, straightens and removes splinters. Without it, destiny will be aborted. The launching point of daddy's shoulders is only achieved after the lifting parent reaches down. To *launch* you must *lift*. To *lift* you must *exert*.

Too often as parents we want someone else to polish and perfect our little arrows.

Arrows must be aimed, so make preparations now to ensure that your children receive a double portion of God's best because of your faithfulness and diligence. Make sure you invest your life to further the Kingdom through the legacy you leave to your descendants.

*Set your heart and soul to help
your children go further and do more
for God than
you have ever dreamed.*

Set your heart and soul to help your children and your grandchildren go further and do more for God than you have ever dreamed. Polish them—lift them! This is God's way of making your life and legacy prosper and bringing to fruition an incorruptible inheritance.

THE GOD FATHER

When you were born into the world, much of what you came to under-stand about God and His creation resulted from observing the people around you. We all learn how to relate to others by observing how our parents and other adults around us relate to one another. We also learn how to handle adversity (or cave in under the pressure) by observing how the adults in our lives handled the challenges that came their way.

Our knowledge of God is literally a composite of the things we've observed and filtered through the lives of others around us. We can never overestimate the power of praying grandmothers, faithful God-fearing uncles and grandfathers who model integrity in business, per-sonal relationships and their dealings with our children.

Only God knows the full impact that our lives make on others, but we can be sure He notices. It seemed to be one of Jesus' chief concerns. He even said:

> Whoever receives one little child like this in My name receives Me. But whoever causes one of these little ones who believe in Me to sin, it would be better for him if a millstone were hung around his neck, and he were drowned in the depth of the sea.[6]

SKEWED, RUDE "FILTERS" MAKE THE WRONG IMPRESSION

Have you ever met an unfriendly or rude resident from a particular city or country? In most cases, we can't help but wonder if *all* the inhabitants of that place share the same traits, opinions and obviously unpleasant manners as the embarrassing ambassador we had the misfortune to meet.

Most of us have heard stories about unfortunate experiences with cab drivers in large cities. Unless those bad experiences are countered by good experiences with more pleasant people from the same city, the "vic-tims" will permanently link their rude experiences with the city and its inhabitants.

In a very real sense, those rude people became filters or translators that colored, or skewed, the impression made about their culture or region.

AMIE DOCKERY

When my husband and I must place our four young children under the temporary care of a child-care provider, I do my best to make sure that that person is capable and trustworthy before I leave. Unfortunately, you never really know how well someone will do until they have the chance to do it.

When I return home, I can easily gauge how the care provider did by checking to see how well he or she cared for my children and maintained the appearance of my home—*in that order.*

A physical house may be in order while the home—the people dwelling in that house, their well-being and their relationships—is in disarray. My children are living beings who require more direct care and attention than my house; so my first concern when I return home is whether or not my children are safe, happy and well fed.

For this reason, I look for a care provider who shares my concern for the well-being of my children. Would you say God is primarily focused on the status of our houses, careers and church buildings or on the well-being of our children (whom He calls His heritage)?[7]

In most cases, our parents become our first and most important filters through whom we see the world and its creator.

Every search for true identity begins and ends with God. If you are searching for your identity on the earth, God is the only forefather you really need to know. First He created a plan, and then He *made you* specifically to fulfill that purpose. He knew you before you were born, and He set you apart before He formed you in your mother's womb.[8]

You were God's idea, so accept it! Once you know the heart of your creator, you will begin to know His purpose for your creation. As you think about all the care God has invested in you, you will want to know Him more and experience Him every day as your Father. You will long to know Him as the creator of your physical body and your eternal destiny.

Parents and mentors have a responsibility to teach their children or students about the things of God. But which is better—to teach them using static one-dimensional representations of the invisible God, or to throw away the copies and share the real thing?

AMIE DOCKERY

You don't come *from* your parents; you come *through* your parents." I have heard my father say this countless times, yet each time I hear these words they have a profound effect on how I perceive myself. My parents greatly influenced who I am and what I have become. When I ponder that simple phrase, however, I realize all over again that I did not come from my parents. I came *from* God *through* my parents. God is my first Father—my creator.

All too often we try to copy what we have in the form of a program or formula and pass it down to our children or to others under our care. Isn't it better to show them how to grow fruit and cultivate a real relationship with God for themselves?

This isn't always the most popular choice because it takes a little work and a lot of faith in God's ability to step in and fill the gap. Wise parents and mentors know they shouldn't step in and take over; their chief role is to guide them gently and encourage them strongly. The Scriptures tell us, "Oh, taste and see that the LORD is good; blessed is the man who trusts in Him!"[9] Teach them to "taste" and to trust!

Once children, new converts or students taste the fruit of God's love and abiding presence, they will no longer be content with mere technical descriptions of what God is like. They will have tasted the real thing and they know for themselves that He is good.

Have you ever met someone who can describe what a relationship with God looks like but has never touched Him or tasted the exquisite richness of His presence? The sad truth is that he or she has settled for a pitiful imitation of the real thing.

Dare to take a risk and entrust your child to God. Yes, you could answer all of his or her questions and keep him or her thoroughly informed with your own personal descriptions. The problem is that information without inspiration—data without a personal encounter with God—won't give your child the breakthrough he or she needs.

It is easier to seek and find the real thing when all substitutes are removed. Your children will be grateful if you refuse to let yourself become a copy but instead point them toward what is authentic. Your personal introduction may leave them hungry to obtain this fruit in their own lives.

Amie Dockery

While researching different methods of education for my children, one specific illustration particularly captured my attention. It came through a school representative who told me that while most schools give children a picture of four apples for them to count, her school actually set four real apples in front of the children.

The simplicity of the idea was extraordinary. She explained that although this method of teaching may be inconvenient and take a little more time than photocopying a sheet of paper, it eliminated a barrier and introduced students to the real thing.

I know from experiences with my own children that tangible fruit has a much greater chance of getting their attention than a piece of white paper. Real fruit speaks for itself. It doesn't need an interpretation or explanation—only an introduction. What does this say about our attempts to introduce our children to God?

Intimate Encounter

Now that we understand where we come from and whom we come through, it is time we know *why*. God created us in His own image and forged a level of intimacy that only He can reach.

A scientific adage states, "Nature abhors a vacuum." The creator of nature also created a vacuum in us, knowing we would be drawn to Him to fill it. It reminds me of the TV infomercials that repeatedly say, "You can't get this anywhere else!"

God has cornered the market on fulfillment for you. He created a space that only He can fill. Then He announced, "You can't get this anywhere else!" Satisfaction begins for us when we find out that what we need does exist and is available. There is one catch, however: He desires a passionate exchange. (If you don't believe this, then offer God a lukewarm drink of passionless praise and wimpy worship and let me know what happens.)

He is asking for intimacy; casual friendship won't do. He isn't seeking mere admirers; He wants sons and daughters. He does not want us to hold Him at arm's length just long enough for a feel-good experience. He wants a marriage, a two-sided commitment for eternity.

Many people feel uncomfortable linking talk of God with discussions of marriage and intimacy, but it was God who chose the marriage relationship to characterize His relationship with the Bride of Christ, the Church.

PASSION DETERMINES WHETHER MARRIAGE IS A PARADISE OR A PRISON

Some see marriage as a paradise and some call it a prison. Those who are distracted and indecisive about love are most likely to view their marriage vow as a prison. But to the one who is deeply and passionately in love, it is a paradise.

AMIE DOCKERY

As a married woman I understand the benefits of a loving marriage relationship. I don't worry about someone coming between my husband and me because there isn't any room for them. No one is closer to me than my husband, and I wouldn't have it any other way. It is paradise to me precisely because there are limitations. It is a lifelong commitment between two parties.

Knowing what you want—an intimate relationship—and trusting the one who can provide it makes all the difference. God knows what He wants and it isn't available in a third person. If you are wondering why, the answer is simple: Only intimate relationships can facilitate reproduction, and God wants to reproduce Himself in us and through us.

A marriage relationship is a rite of passage that you must embrace to experience. It is a covenant relationship that requires you knowingly to eliminate certain levels of interaction with others. Behavior that was fine before the commitment will no longer be acceptable afterward. You simply choose what you want and make no room for what you don't.

All of this sounds foreign to people who view ministry strictly as a lecture directed toward other people from behind a pulpit or as something reserved solely for seminary graduates. It may definitely include these forms of ministry, but all of us are called to *minister to Him, not merely to people.*

BIRTHED THROUGH GOD-WARD PASSION AND SACRIFICIAL PAIN

When Eli the high priest and his sons failed to minister to God properly, the Lord went outside the established pattern of lineage in leadership to install Samuel in their place.[10] Samuel didn't come by the office of high priest and prophet by bloodline alone; he was birthed into it solely through the God-ward passion and sacrificial pain of one desperate woman.

God is still calling people into full-time ministry. He is still selecting many who do not come from a long line of preachers. Many of them were "adopted" by spiritual fathers who lent them their own shoulders to help launch them into their destiny and spiritual inheritance.

Every Christian needs to be mentored in the things of God. In essence, before you can stand on Daddy's shoulders—even the shoulders of an adopted mentor such as Eli—you may have to be birthed out of a mother's prayers and nursed in her lap. This is God's way of mentoring us into ministry. (In other words, you don't have to be born into a preacher's home or stand behind a pulpit for God to consider you a minister.)

GOD CALLED TO SAMUEL AND USED ELI TO CONFIRM IT

Have you ever wondered why God didn't introduce Himself to young Samuel the first time instead of calling his name out *three* times? God wanted to include Eli the priest in the process of introduction. He chose to use Eli (complete with his faults and failures) as Samuel's father figure to affirm what the boy suspected: It was God.[11]

It seems it was just as important for Eli to know that God was talking to Samuel as it was for Samuel to hear God for himself. Yet God also eliminated the "contaminated middleman" using a simple yet profound method—He used Eli's confirmation and instruction to initiate an informal introduction, and from then on Samuel heard and responded to God without any help from Eli. Samuel went on to become one of the greatest prophets Israel ever knew, but it all *began* with one introduction.

Who are you introducing to the voice of God? Can you mentor someone to discern the Master's voice? The next generation might be waiting on your Samuel.

God never intended for ministry and leadership to be reserved or limited solely to what happens behind a pulpit. God is searching for passionate Hannahs who will raise up Samuels, and who will pay the price to keep the fire of worship and passion for God burning. God is looking for Samuels whom He can move into leadership through divine promotion through God-ward passion to God-ordained purpose.

It is amazing to see what desperate Hannah birthed! It is equally incredible to consider what your passionate prayers can birth into your future!

Notes

1. Genesis 18:19, *KJV*.
2. Psalm 68:5, *NIV*.
3. Lance Lambert, *The Uniqueness of Israel* (Eastbourne, East Sussex, UK: Kingsway Publications, Ltd., 1991), p. 106.
4. Ibid., p. 107.
5. Isaiah 49:2, emphasis added.
6. Matthew 18:5-6.
7. See Psalm 127:3, where children are called "an heritage of the LORD" (*KJV*).
8. See Jeremiah 1:5.
9. Psalm 34:8.
10. See 1 Samuel 1—4:1.
11. See 1 Samuel 3:8.

CHAPTER 2

DO THINGS RIGHT, OR DO THE RIGHT THINGS?

It is easy to teach a young boy the proper way to pull out a chair for someone. Yet that same boy may use the right technique to rudely pull a chair out from under a little girl in his class—this is an example of doing something right while doing the wrong thing.

If you survey the horizon of church ministry today, you may notice that many leaders seem to focus on training new converts, seminary students and children how to do things right instead of how to do the right things. They sound the same, but they are not.

We run a serious risk when we major on teaching our children proper religious ritual and theology without also teaching them how to maintain a vital relationship with the One who made them. (By the way, who said we couldn't teach them *all* of these things in proper balance?)

God sent Samuel to *replace* a judge over Israel and his entire priestly family line because they majored on doing things right instead of doing the right things. Eli's sons, Hophni and Phinehas, learned all of the lessons for the mechanics of public ministry in the Holy Place, but they didn't know the truth about the One they worshiped. He is a jealous God who loves people but hates sin and hypocrisy.

PRIESTLY PROCESS WITHOUT PRIESTLY PASSION IS WORTHLESS

Hophni and Phinehas had learned the priestly process but had never received (or had simply rejected) the priestly passion that truly pleases God. They knew how to dress and posture themselves as priests before the public, but they knew nothing about true ministry from the heart before God. It is almost as if Eli had raised his two boys merely to take over the family business as judges, descendants of Aaron and the high priests of Israel. The problem with this approach is that ministry before God is not merely a job; it is a vocation—a *calling with a cost.*

We wouldn't normally think of the priesthood as a business, but if the actions of these two young priests are any guide, then "business" is the best word we could choose for their conduct in the tabernacle at Shiloh.

It is likely that Eli did his best to stress the importance of the duties of the priestly station in Hebrew society, but we have to wonder if he mentioned the importance of ministering to a *holy and righteous God.* As high priest, he probably led Hophni and Phinehas through the same training he had endured to ensure a proper transfer of *priestly protocol and procedure* from generation to generation. But that wasn't enough.

Somewhere along the line the focus of attention made a fatal shift from personal relationship with God to the empty rituals of religious performance in His house. Sadly, this change of perspective poisoned

Eli's relationship with his sons and voided their relationship with God. After it was too late, Eli discovered that the transfer of knowledge had no power to draw his sons into relationship with God. His error was that he had focused on *doing things right* instead of *doing right things*.

The fruit of what Eli sowed was a deadly harvest of hypocrisy, scorn, hard-heartedness and open sin in the very house of God (See 1 Samuel 2:12-17,22). There is something very disturbing about the obnoxious way these two brothers carried out their sin. Sin had become part of their *public* ritual, and it brought shame, ridicule, resentment and divine disfavor on their entire nation. How could anyone have such a lack of reverence for God?

THEY LACKED ACCOUNTABILITY THROUGH RELATIONSHIP

There is overwhelming proof that Hophni and Phinehas were not held accountable for their actions. Accountability can only be established through relationship, and that is where we find the root to many of our own problems today.

The Bible sets the scene and provides clear evidence for the lack of relationship between Eli and his sons:

> Now Eli, who was very old, heard about everything his sons were doing to all Israel and how they slept with the women who served at the entrance to the Tent of Meeting. So he said to them, "Why do you do such things? I hear from all the people about these wicked deeds of yours. No, my sons; *it is not a good report that I hear spreading among the LORD's people.*"[1]

The beginning of this passage leaves us with the sad impression that Eli is very old. It seems odd that this is made so apparent until you realize that this leader of Israel and leading priest had waited until the end of his life to make his sons accountable! We can be sure that Eli loved his sons, but why did this man wait so long to confront them? Sinful behavior like theirs does not show up overnight.

Why did Eli hear about his sons' actions *from others*? This alone proves that he did not know his sons intimately. If he had cultivated a true relationship with his sons, it seems likely that he would have sensed the symptoms of discouragement or unbelief in their lives long before their actions became so well-known.

ELI WAS UPSET ABOUT THE "MEDIA LEAK"

Amazingly enough, there seems to be no proof that Eli knew anything was wrong *until* he heard it through the grapevine! Even in Eli's earnest attempt to bring correction to his sons, we see the glaring value he puts on a bad report "spreading" instead of true concern for his sons' souls. In modern terms, he seemed more concerned that their sins had been "leaked to the media" than over God's response to their sin.

It is no wonder his sons were lost; Eli had missed the point altogether. In all of Eli's wisdom and knowledge, he had managed to cover everything except introducing his sons to God.

God held Eli responsible and accountable for his God-given task as a parent: He was to pass on to his sons the *first commandment with promise*. The first and most important inheritance parents must pass along to their children is the command and privilege to love the Lord with all of their hearts and with all of their strength. This inheritance must be passed on. Without it, everything else loses its worth.

It was in Samuel's very *first* prophetic message—delivered after the third call from the unseen source—that God revealed His plans to correct the intolerable sin of Eli and his sons: the sin of appearing to do everything right while doing all of the wrong things:

> Then the LORD said to Samuel: "Behold, I will do something in Israel at which both ears of everyone who hears it will tingle. In that day I will perform against Eli all that I have spoken concerning his house, from beginning to end. For I have told him that *I will judge his house forever* for the iniquity which he knows, *because his sons made themselves vile, and he did not restrain them*."[2]

Amie Dockery

I am a Houston-born Texan who was raised in a north Dallas suburb. Although I like to visit downtown Dallas, it only happens on special occasions or for business. One time I ventured south to the city for a dear friend's birthday party at a nice Dallas restaurant. When I entered the establishment and began climbing a flight of stairs leading to the party, I suddenly came face-to-face with one of the most famous of all Dallas icons.

This man tipped his Texas-sized cowboy hat and said, "Howdy, darlin'." (He did it in exactly the same way he did on the television show that made the city of Dallas so famous around the world.)

We spoke briefly until my friend walked up to us. She greeted this TV star by saying, "That must have been you pulling up outside in the big black limousine!"

He laughed and nodded as he said without missing a beat, "I have discovered that if I don't spend my money, my heirs will!"

We all laughed at his witty but well-rehearsed response, parted company and headed on to the party. Later on, I took the time to contemplate the man's comment. I had to wonder if he really lived by that motto. Was he really determined to gather and spend all he had without passing something on to the next generation?

How many of us do the same without putting it into words? Surely this is the opposite of God's plan for us and for His kingdom.

DO YOU HONOR YOUR CHILDREN MORE THAN ME?

Earlier, God asked Eli one of the most damning questions a parent will ever hear: "Why do you . . . honor your sons more than Me?"[3] Then the Lord said something that every believer (and especially every Christian leader) should memorize and carry in his or her heart: "Those who honor Me I will honor, and those who despise Me shall be lightly esteemed."[4]

Your life in Christ is not just about going to church or learning and observing some religious ritual. It has nothing to do with saying the right formula or learning the right spiritual equation. You are called and destined to know the source, the reason behind that whole plan and purpose of God. You are called to be joined to *Him*, not merely to a church system. It is our individual covenant bond to God through Jesus Christ that *makes* us the corporate Church.

Somehow the sons of Eli managed to watch what went on in the tabernacle of the Lord without ever having a clue as to the why behind it all. It is as if they believed God didn't really exist.

The Bible calls Eli's sons "corrupt"[5] or "sons of Belial"[6] because they showed no respect for God. They acted as if they were merely caretakers of a museum erected and maintained in honor of long-dead myths and traditions. In their minds, it was a means to a luxurious and powerful lifestyle with few obligations.

Above all, Hophni and Phinehas had no fear of God because they did not know Him. They were supposedly responsible for making offerings to God on behalf of the people, but they merely used and abused the faithful of the Israelite worshipers to fill their own bellies, line their own pockets and satisfy their own lusts.

THEY BULLIED THE PEOPLE
AND STOLE FROM GOD

In the original Hebrew, "Hophni" means "boxer, pugilist, or 'full fists'" and "Phinehas" means "mouth of a serpent."[7] It appears they lived up to their birth names in full. These brothers and their servants bullied the people and took for themselves the very best of the offerings that the people brought to the Lord. They committed adultery with women who gathered in the entrance to the tabernacle, and they caused the Israelites to despise the sacrifices made to God.[8]

Successful mentoring or discipleship is a two-way street. Teachers are only as good or successful as their students. Students, in general, are only as successful as their teachers. Eli's sons sinned because they chose to despise and disrespect the things of God.

According to the Bible, Eli sinned because he permitted the sin to go on and, in effect, honored his sons more than God. Evidently, Eli feared the disapproval of his sons more than he feared the wrath and judgment of God.

If God's kingdom (and your family) is to prosper, then someone must step forward to mentor and guide; and someone has to set themselves to learn. In ideal situations, fathers are the first and greatest mentors of their sons and mothers are the same for their daughters. In our modern age, marked with such a high divorce rate (*in the Church* as well as in the world), there are many homes where this cannot happen. That means someone else in the local church must step up and help fill the void.

You may be a parent who is thinking, *I want to do that for my kids;* or you may be a young adult who is thinking, *My mom and dad aren't doing that. I hate to say it, but I don't think my pastor is doing it either. I need to find somebody who will teach me these truths.*

Have you ever read the Bible account about Eli and his sons and wondered, *What did Eli do different with Samuel that he did not do with his own sons? Where was the mother of Hophni and Phinehas?* (The Bible never mentions her.)

It seems that the only thing Eli provided to Samuel was training in the protocol or procedures and priestly ritual of the tabernacle of the Lord. It was Samuel's mother who prepared the way for God's presence through her passionate prayer. Eli did the initial introduction of Samuel to God's voice, but then God spoke directly to Samuel. Eli simply confirmed it.

ELI PROVIDED PROCEDURE; HANNAH HANDED HIM HER PASSION

Eli taught Samuel the priestly procedures, but Hannah handed down to Samuel her passion toward God. When Samuel came into Eli's life as a young "adopted" son, we see the process of priestly service mixed with the passion of true spiritual worship. At that point it was repackaged and repositioned by God to be carried on to the next generation.

Basically, Eli passed on to his sons the procedures of the hands and head, which are transactions of the flesh. It was Hannah who passed on to her son the passion and protocols of the heart that can only be born of the spirit. It also seems that Eli required things of Samuel that he did not require of his own sons.

It is more difficult to mentor your own children because you "know them after the flesh." They may look like you on the outside, but your overriding desire should be for your children to look like God on the inside.

They may look like you on the outside, but your overriding desire should be for your children to look like God on the inside.

Spiritual reproduction is only successful when we choose to know one another after the spirit, no matter how much we look or act alike in the natural. Could it be that we get so familiar with the "flesh" of our family members that we forget about the treasured spirit within?

Eli had to bear personal responsibility for his mistakes and sins, but he faced one problem that may be common to every parent-child relationship. Familiarity really does breed contempt in many cases. Perhaps this is why the Bible says "a prophet is not without honor except . . . in his own house."[9]

Again, God has divine solutions for human weaknesses. His first solution is to provide family members, such as aunts, uncles, cousins and grandparents, who will echo the same values and principles as a child's parents.

The truth is that many parents don't have access to family members because they are scattered across the continent because of jobs or divorce. God still has a solution called the Church family. The biblical concept of spiritual "adoption" will restore hope to parents and children alike.

JESUS "ADOPTED" 12 MISFITS AND LAUNCHED A REVOLUTION

Moses "adopted" young Joshua as a spiritual son and mentored him into the man and leader who would actually lead Israel across the

AMIE DOCKERY

It can be difficult to mentor your own children, but it isn't impossible. I remember sitting at our kitchen table as a child while my mother mentored other women who knew how to ask the right questions (I was too little to ask those questions at the time). I listened to her answers and I got it somehow. Now I realize that my mother was actually mentoring me as she mentored other people who were drawing wisdom and godly counsel out of her. Under normal circumstances, it would have been impossible for me, as a little child, to ask the deep questions that start such anointed conversations.

I wanted to be one of those whom my mother watered regularly, because I saw those women grow through her mentorship. A hunger grew in me for more teaching when I received mentoring from her in this way. Our relationship in the natural became secondary to the connection we had in the spirit as I grew spiritually.

I don't know how else this would have begun had my mother not used our kitchen table as a place to feed my spirit as well as my flesh.

Jordan and into its destiny. Paul called many of the young leaders of the church his "sons" in the faith and trained them to lead the Church long after he was gone. Jesus "adopted" 12 misfit disciples and launched a revolution. But first, He spent three years mentoring and forming them into a powerful ministry corps that turned the world upside-down in His name.

Just as you may adopt a child, so you can adopt a spiritual son or daughter. In fact, you can even adopt a mentor, if God puts it on your heart. The most important thing to remember in the process is that God wants us all to do *right things*, while He isn't nearly as concerned that we do things right.

Many people want to respond to such remarks about mentoring by citing Paul's statement: "For though you might have ten thousand instructors in Christ, yet you do not have many fathers; for in Christ Jesus I have begotten you through the gospel."[10]

TOMMY TENNEY

I am three generations deep in ministry, but there have been certain times in my life when I knew I needed to be mentored by someone other than my father or my grandfather.

I've made it a practice to choose anointed mentors with proven gifts and abilities in certain areas where I sensed I needed more training or wisdom. At key times in my life, I placed myself at the feet of these men, and their input brought great richness, depth and stability to my life. We all need mentors and teachers, and sometimes we need to go to *them* rather than wait for *them* to come to *us*.

Usually they cite it because they think it discourages mentoring as a New Testament discipleship pattern. Nothing could be further from the truth. Paul was making a point about his particular relationship to the individuals he discipled and the churches he founded; but he was also condoning the work of *many* instructors or mentors in the faith.

When you are called upon to mentor or disciple others, will you place your focus on doing things right or doing the right things?

TOMMY TENNEY

Since I have written many different books over the course of my ministry, Amie Dockery and I entered into a natural mentoring process where I unconsciously mentored her in the writing process. The very pages you are reading are part of that mentoring process. I may be a well-known author at this point, but my desire is to help light that candle and polish the gift in other anointed writers such as Amie.

It will be a great blessing to me if I learn in the years ahead that you or some other reader were so inspired through the impartation and demonstration of mentoring or writing in this book that you went on to accomplish something special in your own life.

Notes

1. 1 Samuel 2:22-24, *NIV*, emphasis added.
2. 1 Samuel 3:11-13, emphasis added.
3. 1 Samuel 2:29.
4. 1 Samuel 2:30.
5. 1 Samuel 2:12.
6. 1 Samuel 2:12, *KJV*.
7. James Strong, *Strong's Exhaustive Concordance of the Bible* (Peabody, MA: Hendrickson Publishers, n.d.), Hebrew #2652, 2651; and #6372, 6310, 5175, respectively.
8. See 1 Samuel 2:15-17,22.
9. Matthew 13:57.
10. 1 Corinthians 4:15.

CHAPTER 3

DEDICATED DOWNSTREAM: LOOSE AND AFLOAT ON GOD'S FAITHFULNESS

Have you noticed that just about the time you run out of options in life, God shows up? How did some of the world's most inconsequential people somehow manage to parent the most influential leaders of all time? What was their secret?

The people in the Bible who parented world changers and nation builders didn't seem to possess some special spiritual status based upon their natural abilities or accumulated knowledge. The evidence implies the opposite. It appears they stumbled upon the secret of God through their *inability* and desperation, not through some virtue of their own.

The story of Moses provides one of the greatest examples of this parental secret in operation:

So Pharaoh commanded all his people, saying, "Every [Hebrew] son who is born you shall cast into the river, and every daughter you shall save alive." And a man of the house of Levi went and took as wife a daughter of Levi. So the woman conceived and bore a son. And when she saw that he was a beautiful child, she hid him three months. But when she could no longer hide him, she took an ark of bulrushes for him, daubed it with asphalt and pitch, put the child in it, and laid it in the reeds by the river's bank.[1]

SAFER IN THE RIVER OF GOD THAN IN HER OWN ARMS

Imagine the feelings that coursed through the heart of Moses' mother. With her son's life threatened by Pharaoh and every Egyptian alert for any sign of Hebrew infants, she decided that her son was safer in the river of God than in her own arms.

Few of us could imagine just how desperate those times were, but we do know it would take desperation for any mother to do what she did that day. Fearing for his life, she prepared a basket, waterproofed it, laid her son inside it and placed him in the river.

The future of her little baby, so innocent and trusting, depended on her decision. Yet she was also in a similar place of vulnerability. She had to trust in God and depend upon Him to deliver her son and spare his life.

Mere words cannot describe the pain and drama of the moment. She must have rehearsed the reasons for her risky decision over and over in her mind. Perhaps her courage wavered as she ventured through the thick reeds to the bank of the River Nile, but then faith and desperation collided and her fingers slipped from the edges of the basket.

Can you imagine the river of anguish that poured from the young mother's heart? Love compelled her to watch helplessly as her firstborn son drifted away from her touch, away from her lullabies and beyond her protection on the crocodile-infested waters of the Nile.

The heartbroken woman silently sobbing on the riverbank that morning couldn't fathom that God had orchestrated those terrible circumstances. Nor could she conceive in her wildest dreams that He would move through her crisis to meet the needs of her family and transform world history in the process. It is amazing how God works out the details in our favor when we dare to trust Him.

> *It is amazing how God works out the details in our favor when we dare to trust Him.*

Even as this mother placed her only son into a basket and committed him to the waters, her sovereign God moved on the heart of Pharaoh's daughter to take her morning bath in the Nile. All of human history literally hinged on the split-second timing needed to join the paths of the Egyptian princess and the Hebrew infant floating along the reed-lined banks of Egypt's most important waterway.

Literally thousands of variables could have upset the delicate balance of destiny—the chance interruption of a royal request, a forgotten article, the passing illness of an attending maiden, the sudden flight of a river loon distracting the inquiring glance of the princess.

NOTHING LESS THAN THE GUIDING HAND OF GOD

It took nothing less than the guiding hand of God to direct the Egyptian princess to the infant in the floating basket. She mentally processed the potential backlash of publicly disobeying her father's royal command to kill all male Hebrew infants, but love and compassion overcame her fear of royal disapproval.

This child would *not* perish on the cold waters of the River Nile. The unfailing current of the river of God carried him into the arms of destiny in just one fateful moment. The destiny of the infant who was later named Moses was preserved beyond all hope. Then Pharaoh's daughter commanded that the child be placed in the arms of a Hebrew nurse—his birth mother—and the deliverer of a nation was saved.

Mere men could never have imagined such a plot. The river of God had cut through seemingly impossible human circumstances to bring two worlds together by divine appointment. The divine river still flows through our lives today.

AMIE DOCKERY

Our family moved to a house with a pool when I was three years old. I already had the reputation for running everywhere I went. My mother says I skipped walking altogether and went directly from crawling to running.

This posed a serious problem when I wanted to play outside near the pool. My parents were concerned that I might get too close to the edge of the pool and fall in, so they knew I had to learn how to swim. I mastered basic swimming skills in my fourth year, but by the next summer I had forgotten that I could swim.

After weeks of trying to convince me I could swim, my parents decided to prove it to me—by throwing me in. My father held me over the pool and I held on for dear life, fearing I would drown. But I also remember *swimming* as soon as I hit the warm water.

My father *knew* I could swim. He wasn't wishing for something that wasn't a reality. He had witnessed the reality the previous year, so he knew I had training and experience to rely on.

My parents recently threw me into another pool that had me wondering whether I would sink or swim. They asked me to speak in the Sunday-morning services at our church while they were out of town. I was extremely reluctant to take the challenge because I wasn't sure I had what it took to bring a word to such a diverse group of people.

Just before the services began, someone asked me, "Are you ready?" To say no would be an insult to my mentors, so I nodded, walked on the stage and delivered what had been invested in me.

I had to trust that what was in me would come forth—I was released to swim. God Himself had planted anointings, callings, His Word and the power of the Holy Spirit in my heart. My parents had faithfully imparted to me wisdom, experience and a passion for God.

When my parents called later that Sunday to see how things went during the services, I thanked my dad again for "throwing me in" and believing I would overcome the fear and swim in God's purposes.

Released into His Destiny on the River of God

Another mother named Hannah also decided to release her only son, Samuel, to the river of God. The Lord had given her Samuel in answer to her passionate prayer. She nursed and nurtured him at home until he was weaned. Then the day came for him to be released into his destiny:

> "I am the woman who stood by you here, praying to the LORD. For this child I prayed, and the LORD has granted me my petition which I asked of Him. Therefore I also have lent him to the LORD; *as long as he lives he shall be lent to the LORD.*" So they *worshiped the LORD* there.[2]

Hannah didn't have any other children at that point in her life. She made a sacrificial choice on a scale similar to Abraham's choice when he offered his only son to God many generations earlier. Yet Hannah kept her covenant agreement with God and passed the supreme test of faith by committing her only son to the river of God's faithfulness.

Perhaps you have come to a time when you, as a parent or mentor, have done all you can do in your own strength and power. Your task at that point is to commit your children or protégés to God's process of destiny. They will be safe if you have ignited the fire of passion and offered them to Him.

(By the way, parent, the Scripture passage that says, "Train up a child in the way he should go, and when he is old he will not depart from it"[3] does not mean a child will never go astray. It is saying that when he reaches maturity he will come back to the source.)

Things May Look Worse Before They Get Better

Is your child floating on the uncertain waters of life right now? Don't worry. Commit him or her to the river of God. You may have to release them to learn their hard lessons.

The story of the prodigal reveals a divine *process*. It reassures us that God is in control, and it warns us that *things may look worse before they get better*. Stand fast in your faith. Commit your child and your dreams for that child to the waters of God's faithfulness. Trust Him to bring your child of destiny safely home in due time.

AMIE DOCKERY

I still remember the day my little brother was dying on the side of the road near our church. I now know how Moses' older sister, Miriam, must have felt as she watched her little brother float away in a thin basket while crocodiles lazed on the riverbank.

Stephen (my brother) was 16 years old at the time he tried to retrieve a volleyball from the street. A large rental truck stopped to let him go by, but a car coming up behind it decided to go around. When my brother stepped out, the car hit him while traveling about 40 miles an hour.

The driver of the car told us that my brother jumped at least three feet in the air. "I don't know how he jumped that quickly, when he saw me," he said. "It happened so fast that I couldn't get my foot from the gas to the brake before I hit him."

The force of the impact shoved my brother's brain against the inside of his skull and triggered massive convulsive seizures. Miraculously, a prank call had been made moments before, summoning an ambulance to a video store next door to the accident scene! They reached my brother even before we did.

More than 200 people gathered around him and prayed before they put him on a Care Flight to Baylor University Hospital. He underwent emergency brain surgery and doctors told us he wouldn't walk for six months—*if he woke up at all*. We were also told he wouldn't talk again until he regained the ability to walk—if it ever happened.

Nine days after the accident, my baby brother woke up and began calling for my mother by name. He walked out of the hospital on the 21st day, and he even played football during his senior year (beginning just two months after the accident)—complete with metal plates in his head.

His miracle was so complete that we have to remind ourselves that it really happened. Since that time my parents have released him to go to college and study abroad in Europe.

It took courage for my mother to do it, but she released my miracle brother to the river of God. She has learned that he is safer in the hands of God than he will ever be in ours.

Plant Them in the Soil of My Faithfulness

The mothers of Moses and Samuel released their children to be dedicated downstream, loose and afloat on God's faithfulness. We all come to that point somewhere, and some of us come to it many times in our lives. Whether you are a parent, mentor, pastor or teacher, the most difficult challenge you will face may come when God says, "Release the ones you love. Yield them to the current of My purposes and plant them in the soil of My faithfulness."

God allows us to mentor others only for a season, and then we must allow them to *graduate* into the hands of the *great* mentor, the Holy Spirit.[4] That is what it means to release them "downstream, loose and afloat on God's faithfulness." No matter how good, gifted and conscientious you are, God's faithfulness is greater than yours, and your greatest security is in His hands.

If you are going through a difficult season at the moment, know that *you are not abandoned.* You may feel as if you are afloat in a small boat on a very big sea, but you are *not* abandoned. Someone holds you in His hands who is bigger than any earthly mentor. You are still in the midst of God's destiny.

When we dedicate our children to the Lord today, the process isn't as dramatic or as black and white for us as it was for Hannah. Even so, we still face some of the same feelings of fear that she faced long ago. The dedication of a child or someone under your influence begins the moment you recognize their calling to minister to the Lord.

Remember that it takes more than a single dramatic act or declaration truly to dedicate someone to the Lord. You *begin* by setting your children apart for a divine purpose, but that initial declaration requires continuous follow-through as they grow and mature. Your role is to provide them with insights into why they were given to God in prayer and how they will be used for the glory of God.

As parents we love to see ourselves in our children. It is natural to see more of our likeness appear in them as they grow and develop. Yet there is another Father who longs to see Himself in them as well.

AMIE DOCKERY

I have heard the story many times. Looking into the faces of my aging father and grandfather I always find the details hard to imagine. At the time of the incident, my father was a six-foot two-inch, muscular seventeen-year-old. He was at that age when he was questioning and testing his father's authority.

Congruent with his independent nature, my dad had done something worthy of punishment. He had never been rebellious or defiant before, but this day would prove to be a turning point in his life.

When my grandfather went in to my father's bedroom to pursue the topic of punishment, he realized that he was physically incapable of disciplining my father. He could no longer enforce rules or punishment on a physical level. If my father chose not to obey, there was nothing my grandfather could do to demand obedience. They both get teary-eyed recalling my grandfather's words.

"Mike, I can't handle you on my own, I am turning you over to God. He knows better than I do how to speak your language and discipline you in the way you will receive."

My father remembers a fear of the Lord coming over him with my grandfather's comments. God definitely knew how to get my father's attention. Within weeks his '55 Chevy looked like an accordion and he was bragging about his brand-new Bible.

He experienced a turnaround that permanently changed his values. God could speak his language. In fact, that was the same year God called him to preach. My grandfather could only deal with the symptoms, but God knew my father's heart. He also knew what circumstances had the greatest potential to change it.

Thirty years later the results of my grandfather's actions are more evident than ever. My grandfather's inability in the natural caused him to release my father to a new level of submission to God.

Every day we must rediscover and renew our commitment to act as *stewards* of our children, while viewing them primarily as sons and daughters *of God* and not merely as our offspring. True dedication requires that we remove ourselves from the equation and yield them to God's training without selfishness.

Trust God to show up each and every time you feel you have run out of options as a parent and mentor. Take courage—you've discovered the secret to parenting. By freely admitting your inability, you have opened

Every day we must rediscover and renew our commitment to act as stewards *of our children, while viewing them primarily as sons and daughters* of God.

the door to God's unlimited ability to carry your children into their true destiny on the river of His faithfulness. Cast them on the waters of divine purpose and watch God move through your children to transform their world and build an eternal Kingdom through your obedience.

Notes

1. Exodus 1:22—2:3.
2. 1 Samuel 1:26-28, emphasis added.
3. Proverbs 22:6.
4. See John 16:13.

CHAPTER 4

TAKING GOD'S FLAME INTO EVERY MAN'S WORLD

Every four years, millions of people watch television coverage of the Olympic torch-lighting ceremony held in Greece. Thousands of volunteers stand by to hand carry the torch through nation after nation as it is transferred from runner to runner until it reaches the nation hosting the Olympic Games.

This torch-passing tradition is said to trace back to the original athletic contests held in ancient Greece in the shadow of Mount Olympus. What a powerful visual picture of the way God imparts His anointing from generation to generation around the world!

God is the source of all anointing and supernatural impartation, but He delights in using *people* to carry the flame of His presence and His unchanging Word throughout human society.

The unity principle behind the passing of the Olympic flame is that *the same flame from one source brings light and unity to countless locations, cultures and generations.* This is the same vision that helped launch one of America's foremost Christian universities. Dr. Oral Roberts dreamed of establishing a full-fledged university that would raise up students who would take the gospel of Christ into every man's world and take God's light where His light is dim. Oral Roberts University is the highly successful product of that dream.

> *Our mandate in the Church is to focus on carrying godly fire wherever we go.*

A similar tradition appears in societies where children (especially sons) are expected to follow in the footsteps of their fathers or parents. In some places where this tradition is extremely legalistic, children are expected to follow *exactly* in their parents' footsteps. Whenever this happens naturally, everything works out. When the children want to branch out or explore another career direction, or vocation, unpleasant consequences often follow.

Our mandate in the Church is to focus on carrying godly fire wherever we go. As long as Christ burns in our hearts, it shouldn't matter where He sends us or how He calls us to spread His light.

What if God plants a different dream or vocation in the hearts of your children? Will you follow earthly traditions or personal desires and force them into vocational boxes they weren't created to fill?

Jesus followed the Jewish tradition of learning his earthly father's trade of carpentry, but He was destined to build a much greater house than one built with wood or stone.[1] Moses was trained and groomed as a prince of Egypt, but he was destined to lead a new nation into its destiny, one without a prince, a king or a political ruler.

Only God knows the gauntlets faced by hundreds of preacher's kids who felt God was leading them into the music world and not into a place behind a pulpit. The same problems often plague the children of highly accomplished parents who have achieved acclaim and position as doctors, attorneys or political leaders.

HE ISN'T A COOKIE-CUTTER GOD

Whether we wear the hat of a parent or of a son or daughter trying to find the way to destiny's door, we must understand that we do not serve a cookie-cutter God. He is the creator, the fountain of unlimited creativity and originality. We shouldn't be surprised if the creator of toucans, hummingbirds and vultures also imparts some originality to us!

Encourage your children to pursue their God-given destiny, even if it takes them to new locations, vocations or career paths far different from yours. God is more interested in your passing on His passion and truth than in preserving mere personal preferences and opinions about minor differences.

The generational inheritance of God is not rooted in some exact position, location or vocation—it is rooted in the realm of the Spirit and in the unchanging truths and principles of God's Word.

If you are a full-time minister, don't blindly require your children to become preachers or evangelists. They may want to carry the power of God's presence into public service or the practice of medicine or law. They may have an anointing from on high to start a business and use the profits to send the gospel around the world. God needs anointed world changers in every walk of life.

WHAT IS THE MOST IMPORTANT THING YOU CAN DO?

As a parent, there are two things you may do to ensure your child's success in God's kingdom: Help your child develop an intimate and loving relationship with God, and impart to them a solid understanding and loyalty to God's Word. Anything beyond these is minor in comparison.

The Moravian community was composed of a mixed lot of people from many different religious traditions, nations and cultures. Their differences—and their loyalty to those differences—made it difficult for them to get along until they began to seek God for *His* opinion and purpose.

God's presence visited them and so transformed them that they became known as a people of prayer. They literally altered the landscape of the Church and the future of entire nations. They became known as "the happy people" in an era when spiritual somberness or seriousness was considered especially holy.

They launched a continuous prayer vigil with teams praying night and day in unbroken succession for more than 100 years. As a result, God began to move on their hearts to take the gospel of Jesus Christ to people who had never heard the good news.

Some of the Moravians were so moved by God that they literally *sold themselves into slavery* just to preach the gospel to slave colonies in the West Indies.

The flame of passion God planted in the Moravians ultimately ignited the hearts of the Wesley brothers in England, who in turn helped launch and fuel great spiritual awakenings in Europe and North America.

CHOICES, FORKED ROADS AND THE DIVINE QUESTION

Too often we approach life as if it were an accident about to happen without rhyme or reason. God doesn't agree. His Word is peppered with eternal destiny, purpose and divine appointments. Life is a series of choices and forked roads awaiting your yes to every divine question. God said:

> For I know the thoughts that I think toward you, says the LORD, thoughts of peace and not of evil, to give you a future and a hope. Then you will call upon Me and go and pray to Me, and I will listen to you. And you will seek Me and find Me, when you search for Me with all your heart.[2]

For You formed my inward parts; You covered me in my mother's womb. I will praise You, for I am fearfully and wonderfully made; marvelous are Your works, and that my soul knows very well. My frame was not hidden from You, when I was made in secret, and skillfully wrought in the lowest parts of the earth. Your eyes saw my substance, being yet unformed. And in Your book they all were written, the days fashioned for me, when as yet there were none of them.[3]

Some of us emerge from the womb and immediately charge toward our divine destiny (this is a good description of John the Baptist).

ORDAINED TO BE A PIONEER

John's father was a priest and his mother was descended from Aaron, the first high priest, but John was not destined for the traditional priesthood.[4] He was ordained from the womb to be a pioneer who would usher in a whole different epoch in the kingdom of God.

John the Baptist would be on nearly everyone's shortlist for the most passionate man in the Bible. He was wild and original in his enthusiasm. John served the same God his father served, but he was destined to do it in a totally different (and very unorthodox) way.

In retrospect, it almost seems that the angelic warning to John's father, Zacharias, to keep his son from wine was meant to avoid alcohol being blamed for John's dramatic behavior in later years. What a package John was! He was a shock from the moment Gabriel announced to Zacharias that he was on the way.[5]

While Zacharias was burning incense in the most holy place, an angel appeared and told him that his barren wife would bear a son, and his name would be John (and Zacharias was unable to speak until after the baby was born).

Eight days after the child's birth, he was taken to the temple to be circumcised. Family members assumed he would be named Zacharias according to tradition, but his mother spoke up and said, "No! He is to be called John." When Zacharias nodded in agreement, he finally regained his ability to speak.

It must have surprised the crowd when Zacharias did not give John a Levitical family name. Names symbolized a person's heritage and were thought to predict their destiny. Everyone assumed John would be a priest in the family tradition (one of the highest-ranking vocations in that day). They were wrong. God had something else in mind.

WHAT KIND OF CHILD WILL THIS BE?

The unusual events surrounding John's conception, birth and circumcision pointed to the possibility that God would use him to do something new. The Bible says everyone left that day wondering, "What kind of child will this be?"[6]

The passion of God may lead some of us to continue in the path of our family lineage. God may anoint others to inject something new into the generational heritage. John already had a priestly spiritual heritage through his parents, but he was destined to receive the prophetic mantle of Elijah through the Spirit of God.[7]

It seems safe to assume that John felt the pressures of living in the home of a high priest. He knew that tradition dictated he would become one of the most powerful men in Israel by default. Yet it seems he also knew he would have to take a leap of faith and at some point break away from tradition to fulfill his destiny.

Imagine how John the Baptist must have felt: One day he would have to tell his peers and the ruling elders and priests (his father's closest friends) that he would *not* pick up where his father left off. He would face heavy judgment, because no one would understand how he could reject such an honorable birth and lofty vocation.

POTENCY AND PURITY THROUGH PRESSURE

John felt the pressure of his destiny pressing against the force of human traditions and expectations. Few of us desire such pressure, but it is nearly always productive. Pressure releases the sweetest fragrance from a flower, the finest juice from a grape and the purest oil from an olive. A human "vessel" under pressure may experience discomfort, but it usually produces potency and purity within.

The diamond is nature's best example illustrating the combined power of pressure and heat on a basic element (carbon). The element that constitutes coal and a diamond is the same. The only difference is that the diamond was subjected to the forces of incredible pressure and heat that fundamentally changed its value, characteristics and appearance.

The diamond is the clearest and most beautiful of all precious stones, yet we call something "coal-black" to emphasize how dark it is. We burn the carbon molecules in coal to produce electricity and heat our homes, but we treasure the carbon molecules in the form of a diamond. It is passage through great pressure and heat that makes the critical difference.

Can you imagine the kind of pressure and heat it takes to transform one of nature's blackest and softest elements into a crystal-clear stone ranked as one of the hardest and most dense of all naturally occurring substances?

The pressure of destiny in our lives accomplishes the same thing. Diamonds are formed through the pressure and heat of volcanic action or the mass of the earth's outer layers. Great Christians are produced through the pressures created by people, circumstances, God and human weaknesses.

We think very little about what John the Baptist faced in the years he was still at home with his parents, so it is easy to forget that John didn't know how everything was going to turn out. John was a great prophet, but he was still a human being who probably wanted to flee the situation at times. Yet he was keenly aware of his divine destiny, and he knew he had to be sure he followed the will and timing of God.

HE WOULD SEE THE GLORY IN A NEW WAY

John's purpose was to prepare Israel for the coming of the Messiah. He was a living bridge between the ancient system of animal sacrifices and a new spiritual priesthood in the kingdom of God established by Jesus Christ.

The life and ministry of John the Baptist presents a powerful lesson about spiritual inheritance. John would never see behind the veil as his father did, but He would see the visible glory of God in a new way, embodied in the flesh of Jesus Christ. As a prophet he saw many things before they took place.

According to the traditions of men, John the Baptist was next in line as high priest, but God called him to carry his passion outside of the cities and temples built by men. He exchanged the elaborate robes and ephod of a priest for the camel's hair clothing of a prophet, and he fanned the fires of revival from the wilderness rather than in the courts of the temple.

You may charge into your destiny from birth as John did, or you may follow the only path you know to take until God arrests you in divine confrontation and launches you in the specific direction of His choosing. This perfectly describes the life and ministry of Saul the Pharisee, who became Paul the apostle. It only took a 30-second encounter with God on the road to Damascus to change everything in his life.

You Can't Get There from Here

One day a young man realized he was lost and decided to stop for directions. He searched among all the farms, fields and detours until he finally spotted an old farmer walking down the road.

He pulled up alongside him, rolled down the window and asked the man for directions. After the young man explained exactly where he was headed, the old man hung his head to ponder the situation.

"Well you go up to the end of the street and . . . uh, no that's not right. Let me think," he said. "Oh, I know. Take this road west and then turn . . . well, no, that's not right either."

The young man was pretty sure by this point that he should have asked someone else, but the old man interrupted his thoughts by saying, "You know son, *I don't think you can get there from here.*"

Have you ever felt as if you couldn't reach your destiny from where you were? If you dwell on the details, the "ifs" can become overwhelming.

Many of God's champions in the Bible began their journey on one path and ended up on another because God changed their motivation and gave them vision.

Consider Jacob, Isaac's son. His chief passion early in his life was to get all he could and take care of number one (even if it meant swindling his own family members). Midway through life he experienced a life-changing encounter with God that transformed him from a swindler into a patriarch of honor. God personally changed his name from Jacob to Israel to mirror his true spiritual destiny as one of the great patriarchs of the Bible.

JESUS DID NOT LIMIT HIS MINISTRY TO TEMPLES AND SYNAGOGUES

Countless streams of ministry are not normally accepted in the minds of many Christians, but God has made it clear that He wants us to invade every area of life with His light.

Traditional ministry methods would have limited the ministry of Jesus to temples, synagogues and other religious places of worship or scholarship. His religious peers could not understand why Jesus spent most of His time among sinners in the cities, in the country and even in their homes. We still marvel that Jesus formed His 12-man ministry team using unlearned fishermen, tax collectors and other recruits from everywhere *except* the priesthood and the religious elite.

Rich Marshall, founder of ROI, an inspirational and equipping ministry to the business community, notes on the back cover of his book *God@Work*:

God is showing up in places we have never imagined. We thought He was just for Sunday church or mid-week Bible study. But God is showing up in small businesses and on construction sites, in schools and in politics. He is in factories and at check-out counters, at nurses' stations and the stock exchange. God is showing up everywhere outside of where we expect Him to be.[8]

The Church is discovering that God is far more creative than we ever wanted to believe. He packages His life, light and power in the form of opera singers, commodities traders, retail store managers, neurologists, civil engineers, auto mechanics, tool and die craftsmen, carpenters (we should have guessed this one), schoolteachers and virtually every other legal occupation not related to sin.

> *Wherever He finds us, the Lord calls us to the generational fishing hole, hands us a fishing pole and slaps a Follow Me sign on our back.*

He has even used *entertainers* and *sports figures*—and ministry never looked so good or reached so many.

AMIE DOCKERY

I learned during an African safari about how God simplifies parenting for wild animals. Our safari guide pointed out various markings on specific animals and called them Follow Me signs.

The African lions had black hair on the back of their ears. The ears of leopards were marked as well, and their tails also featured a white tip. The antelope, deer and gazelle we saw each carried different versions of a distinctive black and white stripe pattern on the backs of their front and rear legs and on their tails.

These dramatic and vivid markings are located on the backside of each creature, and their purpose is to help the offspring of each species follow their parents despite their highly camouflaged environment.

It was especially interesting to see how God placed each marking directly at eye level for the little ones of each species. An adult lion could be easily hidden from its offspring while crouching in the grass during a hunt, but God made the back of a lion's ears a distinctly different color from the rest of its body, and those ears are the highest point of its body when it is on the prowl.

An adult leopard waves its tail around like an energetic tour guide waving a sign to lead a group through a crowded building. The white fluff at the end of the leopard's tail bobs around directly in front of the cubs to keep them from being distracted or possibly getting lost.

The markings of antelope, deer and gazelles are placed lower down on the legs. These markings not only direct the young toward safety, but they also provide highly visible directional arrows pointing toward the source of the mother's milk.

The creator designed these natural Follow Me signs in clear, distinct and highly contrasting patterns of black and white. Even in our human environment, it seems easier for children to detect and follow distinctive signals, symbols or communications in black and white patterns.

Your individuality is marked by your personality and lifestyle, but your identity is marked by the way you live and relate to God and the world around you. I've noticed that many parents seem to save the most colorful side of their personalities for private display among friends. The rest of the time they just seem to blend in with the popular culture and rarely display leadership or make any effort to train their children for success.

Is it any wonder that so many children get lost in the confusing jungle of life? They don't know who or what to follow. Are we leaving our children clear Follow Me signs to guide them in their spiritual path? What signals are we sending backward in their direction?

Would anyone want to follow *you* based upon the signs they see in your life? Do you share your most distinctive traits and leadership gifts with your children, or do you reserve them for adult company? Have you shown them how to journey through life's jungle in good times and in bad? Finally, when your children draw close to you, are they rewarded with warm and welcoming refreshment or with stern warnings to leave you alone?

Most species in the animal world do these things automatically, but we must make a *choice*. We must make sure we leave clear guidelines and provide vital survival training for our children.

God has called us to carry His flame into our office buildings, shopping malls, community centers and neighborhoods. He has commissioned us to feed the inner lamp of His glory in crisis-filled hospital corridors and to teach our children how to do the same. This is no call for compromise; it takes God-given courage and determination to fan the holy flame of God-ward passion from generation to generation and in different locations and vocations.

God is looking for "fishers of men"[9] from every walk of life. Have you noticed that it often takes a fisherman to reach a fisherman and a dockworker to reach a dockworker? Wherever He finds us, the Lord calls us to the generational fishing hole, hands us a fishing pole and slaps a Follow Me sign on our back (and the first fishing assignment usually takes place *in our own homes*).

HE PURSUED HIS PASSION TO PLEASE THE FATHER

The most powerful "bait" in our fishing arsenal is our passion for God and His power at work in our lives. That is why our greatest passion must be to please God in all that we say and do. Unfortunately, this doesn't come naturally.

Jesus pursued His passion to please the Father to the fullest, even though He was tempted and distracted in the same way you and I are. He didn't fail or fall short, and He will help us do the same if we give Him access to our hearts.

God anointed us to pursue divine purpose with holy passion. Even in our fallen state, we tend to be passionate about favorite concepts or personal convictions. With very little effort, most of us could compile quite a list of passions operating in our lives over the years: Defend the underdog. Speak the truth. Care for the unfortunate. Preach the gospel. Live another day. Generate income. Procreate. Travel. Have meaningful relationships.

The list could go on, but you get the point. Everyone has a passion. Perhaps your passion was birthed while you listened to your father's tales of injustice. You may have stumbled upon some wrong or great need that motivated you to make a difference or take up a cause. Whatever the case, passion helps us fulfill the divine purpose for our lives.

AMIE DOCKERY

Our family meets on a regular basis to discuss our personal dreams and immediate goals for the future. We cover every topic from college classes to vintage cars, church-building programs, staff repositioning and future ministry opportunities.

We may not put anything on paper, but together we are gaining a broader view of how our dreams, desires and destinies are intertwined.

These meetings helped to introduce me to my destiny as a daughter. They also answered one of my lifelong questions: What would it have been like to be friends with my parents when they were my age?

As with so many other children, I often asked myself this question whenever I longed to see them dreamy eyed instead of worried over some pressing problem.

In our daily lives, we usually base our relationships on stages of accomplishment. In the world of dreams, we are all the same age because we are eternally young at heart. When we dare to dream together, we level the playing field, because we are all speaking of things we hope to do rather than things we have already accomplished.

When we dream out loud as a family, our future reverberates with giddy laughter punctuated by triumphant high fives.

We are literally experiencing a dream come true as we pursue lives of ministry and service together in Christ. It is especially thrilling to hear your parent express excitement over the details of one of their dreams in the making—especially when you know it's *you!*

As Christians, we must put all passions and convictions under the overriding priority of following Jesus Christ, our first love. No matter what we do in life, and no matter how we do it or where we pursue it, this truth should influence every decision we make:

For you were bought at a price; therefore glorify God in your body and in your spirit, which are God's.[10]

You were bought at a price; do not become slaves of men.[11]

Divine purpose and passion for deity go hand in hand. This isn't theory—it must become a reality. It is unhealthy for misdirected passion to win out over divine purpose, and it is very unlikely to please God. On the other hand, purpose without passion is fruitless.

AMIE DOCKERY

When my parents started our church in 1976, they were equipped to pioneer. Many others just like them started off on their own to build something out of nothing. They fulfilled the mandate for their generation. The grace of God covered that era and brought worldwide success in founding new works for the Kingdom.

However, what once required a shovel, concrete and wood, now requires the tools and skills of a finishing carpenter. Precise measurements, angle saws and technical expertise have replaced the ripsaws and hammer guns of house framers.

I have found that the tools for the trade change, as do the times. Years ago the details of Christian education or implementation of specific visions and administration were not addressed. Today, times have changed, and so have the opportunities we have to reach our world.

When I was a child, we passed out gospel tracts door-to-door. In the last decade I have seen graphic artists invite thousands to church with one stroke of design on an Internet page. The public Internet didn't even exist when our church was founded.

The lines of ministry have been broadened because where *there are people there are platforms*. Present and future generations must continually sharpen their tools and clearly define and pursue their calling within the kingdoms of this world. This is the way we make them the kingdoms of our God. He seeks trustworthy, knowledgeable heirs to whom He can transfer the wealth of the world.

It is vital that you properly identify your purpose, so you can effectively focus your passion. Those best equipped to help you identify your purpose and focus your passion are those who went before you and who have a personal interest in your success. This includes parents, godly mentors and proven leaders exhibiting godly character and accomplishment in Christ. This is God's way of advancing His kingdom from generation to generation: He disperses the same holy flame in many different locations and vocations.

Notes

1. See Mark 6:3. Evidently Jesus did more than simply learn his father's trade. Mark mentioned in his Gospel that Jesus was known as a carpenter by those in His home-town, but there is no mention of Joseph. It appears that he had died earlier and that Jesus took over the family business and supported the family through the labor of His hands. It is also probable that He taught His younger half-brothers the family trade as well. Yet He was destined for a totally different calling.
2. Jeremiah 29:11-13.
3. Psalm 139:13-16.
4. See Luke 1:5.
5. See Luke 1:11-20.
6. Luke 1:66.
7. See Luke 1:17.
8. Rich Marshall, God@Work (Shippensburg, PA: Destiny Image Publishers, Inc., 2000), n.p.
9. Matthew 4:19, NIV.
10. 1 Corinthians 6:20.
11. 1 Corinthians 7:23.

CHAPTER 5

DON'T START OVER—PRESERVE, MULTIPLY AND PASS IT ON!

Many families in America seem to *start over* again with every new generation. In contrast, certain groups with strong family relationships, including many Jewish, Japanese, Vietnamese and Korean families, demonstrate an uncanny ability to transfer family wealth, knowledge and religious values smoothly from generation to generation.

God has always intended for His people to operate this way on an even greater scale in both the natural and supernatural realms. Jesus and Paul said as much to their disciples:

Jesus said:

Most assuredly, I say to you, he who believes in Me, the works that I do he will do also; and greater works than these he will do, because I go to My Father.[1]

And the glory which You gave Me I have given them, that they may be one just as We are one: I in them, and You in Me; that they may be made perfect in one, and that the world may know that You have sent Me, and have loved them as You have loved Me.[2]

Paul the apostle said:
The things which you learned and received and heard and saw in me, these do, and the God of peace will be with you.[3]

These passages reveal the higher perspective of God for our lives and the future. We are limited by time, living between the temporarily fixed boundaries of the moment and the place. In other words, it is difficult for us to think about how things will be 10 years from now when we are wrestling with a problem today.

From God's perspective, everything is *now*. He sees the end from the beginning, and He is surprised by nothing. We need the security offered by God's higher perspective to fulfill our calling from generation to generation.

TOMMY TENNEY

I noticed that when I would get on a crowded elevator with my daughters, especially when they were four or five years old, they would say, "Pick me up, Daddy."

Have you ever imagined what a child's view is like on an elevator? All they can see are people's backsides. What they're saying is, "I don't like the way it looks from down here."

From their low-level perspective, it made them feel claustrophobic. Daddy's perspective in the crowded elevator made them feel better because it allowed them to see things from a higher perspective.[4]

God is more interested in continuous building than in rebuilding. He wants us to accumulate and preserve the spiritual treasures He gives us and pass them on as foundations upon which future generations may build.

It is as if a secret war is raging within and against human civilization. This conflict *interrupts* the intergenerational transfer of everything that really matters. War and internal conflict tend to destroy a nation's cities, decimate its economy, dissipate its energies and divide its people. This must *not* happen in the Church.

Will the Chain Be Unbroken?

War and continual strife force nations to expend resources and lay aside plans for growth and advancement. Any hopes for newer and better buildings, roads, industrial development and the infrastructure of a healthy economy dissolve in the heat of battle. Families lay aside dreams of nicer homes or new purchases.

Any nation or family trapped in a war must remain in the shadow lands of rebuilding things that have been destroyed or lost. This is how strife threatens the transfer and exchange from one generation to the next. Hopes of continuous building and growth from generation to generation quickly fade under the shadow of war and strife.

Spiritual war or *division* is especially destructive to our spiritual inheritance and the transfer of Kingdom purpose from generation to generation. Satan aims to keep God's kingdom from growing by instigating strife and division. This dissipates our energies and creates a need for constant healing and rebuilding instead of continuous building in unity and power.

Yes, we manage to pass along *some* things from generation to generation, but most of the time we pass along *empty ritual* instead of vibrant truth and intimate relationship with God.

A young mother was making Christmas dinner while carefully following the family tradition of cutting off one end of the Christmas ham. She called in her mother and asked, "Mom, why did you always cut off the end of the Christmas ham when I was a kid?"

"I don't know, honey. Let's ask Grandma. I learned how to prepare ham by watching her cook when I was a little girl. I think it is part of the secret to Grandma's family ham recipe."

When they called Grandma into the kitchen and asked her about the family tradition of cutting off the end of the ham, she just laughed and shook her head. "No, there's no secret recipe or trick to the technique. The only reason I cut off the end of the ham was because my broiling pan was too short."

Empty tradition often masquerades as deep knowledge in one's life, even in one's Christian life.

IN ALL YOUR GETTING, GET UNDERSTANDING

How often do we pass down ritual without knowledge, wisdom and understanding? The Bible says, "Wisdom is the principal thing; therefore get wisdom. And in all your getting, get understanding."[5]

If the next generation understands *why* we do what we do as God chasers pursuing His purposes, then they are likely to make the right choices for all the right reasons long after we are gone.

If the next generation understands why *we do what we do as God chasers pursuing His purposes, then they are likely to make the right choices for all the right reasons long after we are gone.*

We need the godly knowledge and experiences of previous generations to help guide later generations in their journey into God's purposes. This is underscored in the lives of the children of Israel who escaped Egyptian bondage and journeyed to the Promised Land.

The *first generation* of Hebrews whom God dramatically delivered from slavery under Pharaoh knew the sting of the taskmaster's lash. They felt the fear inspired by the deadly plagues God sent upon Egypt, and they had the thrill of seeing God divide the Red Sea in front of their eyes. They witnessed the destruction of Egypt's elite charioteers, and they ate manna in the desert. Yet in the end, their unbelief led to their undoing.

What Has God Done for Us?

The *second generation* of Israelites were born free in the wilderness, so they didn't know how bad things had been under Pharaoh's cruel rule. Second generation people tend to wonder, *What is so great about being a child of God? What has He done for us?*

Amie Dockery

A similar Exodus experience occurred in my own family. My great-grandparents were good people and they had raised my paternal grandparents. But my grandparents did not experience the power of God until after they visited a different kind of church. My grandparents' (and my great-grandparents') lives were forever changed in the one dramatic moment when they received the truth. They passionately pursued their call and became ministers soon afterward—and they continue to preach the gospel to this day.

My father was a *third-generation* believer who was baptized in the Spirit at the age of eight. My brother and I gave our hearts to the Lord at an even younger age, and we became the *fourth generation* in our family to serve God. Although our age of personal dedication began earlier with each generation, we have found that those who are "born" into freedom face their own unique challenges.

While first-generation believers often experience a dramatic conversion from darkness to light that creates a monumental line in the sand in their lives, second- and third-generation Christians generally don't. They may even feel ashamed because they don't have a dramatic testimony of darkness into light.

My grandparents marched away from their past and into a bright future with God. Although I repented of my sins and was saved, I didn't feel "removed" from anything. My decision to serve the Lord didn't divide my past from my future or dramatically alter my lifestyle as it had for my ancestors. I was raised in a home filled with the love of Jesus, so I found myself asking, "From what was I saved?"

The second generation of Hebrews born during the wilderness journey had no memory of the great Exodus from Egypt or the crossing of the Red Sea. They had heard the oral traditions and stories handed down from their parents and the community, but life for them was limited to the endless monotony of desert sand and the subtly natural appearance of what was actually *divine provision*.

STARTING IN A BETTER PLACE ON A NEW FOUNDATION

The second generation started out in a better place than their parents did, but only because their parents followed Moses to freedom and became the foundation of a new Jewish nation.

It was the first generation that received the Law and the divine promise of land on the other side of the Jordan, and later entered into a unique covenant relationship with God, marked by the circumcision of every male as a physical sign of separation.

The first generation experienced the miraculous first and entered the covenant later. The second generation entered the covenant first and then embarked on a supernatural journey of their own during which they would come to know the God of Abraham, Isaac and Jacob for themselves (and discover their own human limitations in the process).

It seems especially significant that at the end of the wilderness journey, God said Moses' role was over and appointed Joshua to take the second generation into the Promised Land. It took the faithfulness of *both mentors* to get the job done.

In Joshua 5:7, God specifically called out the second generation, the one born in the wilderness. "For they were uncircumcised, because they had not been circumcised *on the way*" (emphasis added).

The first generation of the children of Israel became so absorbed in their movement through the wilderness that they forgot to circumcise their children "on the way" or in the process. (We face a similar problem today. We are so absorbed with the struggle and process of life that we have neglected to introduce our children to the living God who redeemed us from bondage.)

When the second generation was circumcised, Joshua said that God rolled back "the reproach of Egypt."[6] Why would God say that about a

TOMMY TENNEY

One weekend, when both my wife and I were out of town, our youngest daughter (who was nine years old at the time) took it upon herself to choreograph a dance and teach four other children the movements. Then she told our local pastor that she had a dance her group would like to perform for the congregation, and he told them to be ready.

We received numerous telephone calls informing us that our daughter's young dance troupe had "brought the house down." She had repeatedly told me, "Daddy, I can dance." She hadn't taken any dance lessons, but I nodded my fatherly approval to encourage her. The truth is that I had no idea what was really in her.

Staff members who watched the girls dance told me, "This wasn't just some cute little-girl performance. She had the interpretative moves down, and she taught all of the other kids to do them too." (Now she's taking dancing lessons—in the advanced class.)

I still pictured my daughter as a toddler or a young girl standing on my toes while I danced around the room. My kids laugh and say I resemble a dancing bear because I can't dance. But *at one point*, I could dance better than my little daughter. Today my little girl has other mentors who will take her further than I ever could. What began with me must now be carried forward by others.

Sometimes those around you need only a lift to see higher than they can on their own. Little girls start by dancing on Daddy's feet, and little boys begin by dancing cheek to cheek with Mother. In due time they will teach others. It is a beautiful picture of the way our heavenly Father lifts us into the heavenlies to give us a God's-eye view of things so that we can fulfill His purpose.[7]

generation born into freedom? That generation had never lived in Egypt or been tainted by slavery. The truth is that God is speaking of something spiritual, not natural.

The physical act of circumcision was required to remove something they were *born with*, not something that had attached itself through a *life experience*.

When God delivered the Israelites from Pharaoh, He rescued them from physical bondage. When He gave them the opportunity to enter into a personal covenant relationship with Him, He was saving them from spiritual bondage.

WE NEED PASSIONATE RELATIONSHIP, NOT PASSIONLESS RITUAL

Circumcision in biblical times represented a permanent outward mark signifying an eternal covenant that set the Israelites apart as God's people. In our day, wedding bands also represent an outward sign signifying a permanent earthly covenant or vow of fidelity.

Does a wedding band make you married? No, anyone can buy one or put a band on their finger. A wedding ring serves only as an outward reminder or sign of a sacred relationship of the heart.

The second generation was not rewarded with the Promised Land until *after* they stated their loyalty to God. They couldn't enter in simply because their parents had entered a covenant in the wilderness. God required them to enter in to a covenant *themselves*.

Jesus offered His life on the cross to save all of us from our sins, but He forces His will and saving grace on no one. Each of us must *choose* to submit our will to God and acknowledge Jesus as Lord and Savior before we can enjoy the benefits of His salvation.

Outward transfers of power and possessions are not enough. When we fail to pass along both the knowledge and the God-ward passion of our lives to our children, we put their future in jeopardy.

The importance of intergenerational transfer is a fact of history. The empire of Mali dominated West Africa from the early thirteenth century to the late fifteenth century. Formerly a state within the empire of Ghana, Mali rose to greatness after Ghana fell under the pressure of invading forces and internal disputes.

Mali prospered under the leadership of Sundiata, the Lion King, and another great leader named Mansa Musa. After his death, however, his sons could not hold the empire together.

As Mali's power waned, the trade center of Songhai asserted its independence and rose to power within Mali's former empire. Great Songhai kings extended the Songhai kingdom farther than Ghana or Mali had before it. It became the largest kingdom in medieval West Africa, but the riches of its gold and salt mines led to an attack by an invading army from Morocco. The Songhai empire, *already weakened by internal political struggles*, went into decline.[8]

We must learn how to concentrate, duplicate, multiply and transfer the spiritual wealth, knowledge and passion of God's presence in our lives to future generations. Otherwise, they will be doomed to start over, rediscover, rebuild and reestablish themselves in Christ at great cost and needless pain.

TOMMY TENNEY

Wales is home to some of the most passionate people on Earth. Located in southwestern Great Britain and bordering the Irish Sea, Wales is ruggedly beautiful, but its inclement weather is almost legendary.

If you ask the average American to describe something remarkable about Wales, they might mention the Prince of Wales or the famous Welsh singing tradition.

There is one remarkable tradition in Wales that is a mystery even to most of its residents. If you attend the typical Welsh rugby match today, you may or may not be impressed with the skill of the teams. But you are almost certain to be surprised by the singing.

No, it isn't because of the legendary Welsh tenors. In fact, the singing may be below par because many of the men are likely to be tipsy from excessive drinking. The mystery and the wonder are found in *what* the men sing at the start of every game.

In sunshine and in rain, drunk or sober, the rugby players of Wales pause before every game to sing a *hymn* passionately! The hymn of choice is commonly called "Bread of Heaven," but its true title is "Guide Me, O Thou Great Jehovah," and it was written by William Williams. It includes the words, "Bread of Heaven, feed me now and ever more." (If a team does well, its players often repeat their rendition of "Bread of Heaven" during or after a match.)

Why would mostly drunken competitors in a public athletic match sing such a powerful hymn with passion so intense that tears flow freely from singers and spectators alike? Sadly, it is the last remnant of the Welsh revival that began in 1904. The music lived on, but the *passion for God that inspired it* didn't cross the generation line.

That passion was so great that worship once permeated Welsh society early in the twentieth century. It is said that the people of Wales during that time could not bear to go very long without worshiping God.

The people of Wales shopped, sold goods, worked at their trades, labored in the coal mines and played their beloved rugby as usual—but spontaneous outbreaks of passionate worship became the norm throughout the land. They couldn't even complete a rugby match without breaking out into spontaneous and passionate worship to God.

Except for a few notable exceptions, this outward marker of God-ward passion possessed by a previous generation has become an empty tradition for today's generation. The hymn appears to have lost the essence of its meaning; nevertheless, drunken spectators and players stand at every rugby match to sing "Bread of Heaven, feed me now and ever more."

At the right time and place, God will redig the well of Welsh passion for God and lead the lost members of this generation to Himself. Yet I still wonder what might have happened had the previous generation successfully passed on their spiritual vigor and passionate love for God to their children and their children's children.

How Do You Pass Your Best to the Next Generation?

Whether or not we want to admit it, we all face a challenge: *How may we pass along our precious knowledge, experiences, skills and wisdom to the next generation?*

How many skills and techniques perfected in previous generations are totally lost to us today? How much accumulated knowledge has been squandered away by uncaring and unconnected ancestors and predecessors over the years?

The world is filled with examples of past artistic and creative achievement that cannot be easily duplicated today because the generational transfer of knowledge and passion failed or was tragically interrupted.

The Link Was Broken and Knowledge Was Lost for 1,000 Years

Collectors around the world pay top dollar for fine porcelain crafted during China's Ming dynasty between 1368 and 1644, yet few Westerners realize why the craftsmanship and culture of that dynasty is so special. The Ming era was marked by the return of Chinese rule and the *restoration* of many ancient Chinese traditions *lost* in previous generations under Mongol rule.[9]

Medieval swordsmen treasured blades of Damascus steel because of their unprecedented strength, lightness, sharp cutting edge and the distinctive wood-grain pattern on their surface. Due to these unique qualities, Damascus steel was one of the marvels of the medieval Middle East.

It also posed a difficult problem for historians and archaeologists until recent years because this kind of steel can only be made using a highly advanced co-fusion process thought to be *distinctly modern.*

However, archaeologists have recently unearthed evidence indicating that ancient metalworkers developed Damascus steel by learning how to melt together (co-fuse) low-carbon iron with high-carbon iron. They did it using thick-walled air-driven clay furnaces capable of producing temperatures as high as 2,500 degrees Farenheit.[10]

Somehow, the generational link was broken. This advanced fusion technique from antiquity was lost to the world until modern metallurgists finally rediscovered the technique *nearly 1,000 years later!*

Human history is filled with sad stories of expertise carefully and painfully developed by preceding generations somehow being dropped to the ground or forgotten by succeeding generations. This often pointed to the demise of the culture that developed the expertise in the first place. It happened to ancient Egypt, to Greece, to Rome and even to the Church birthed in the first century.

World history reads like an accident report, revealing the splendor and unspeakable tragedy of knowledge lost and civilizations collapsed under the weight of moral depravity and the ravages of warfare.

God never intended for His people to suffer that fate. We must preserve the wisdom, knowledge and passion for God that we've received from previous generations. This will equip us to eliminate the mistakes and take possession of our inheritance in Christ.

AMIE DOCKERY

During my travels in Europe, I learned that Rome began construction on its ancient Colosseum shortly after A.D. 70, and the Emperor Titus opened it just 10 years later. The Colosseum featured a brilliant white marble façade and was adorned with golden statues. It is said that 40,000 slaves worked 24 hours a day for eight ~~years to finish the project so quickly.~~

Today we remember the Colosseum more for its bloody history than for anything else. Gladiators or interspecies combat killed an estimated 5,000 animals to entertain audiences in the opening ceremonies alone! Later on, spectators cheered as Christians were mocked, tortured and martyred within its walls.

About 400 years later, the Emperor Constantine (306-337) ordered the construction of a grandiose basilica in Rome to honor Peter, the prince of the apostles. It was completed around A.D. 349 but was virtually in ruins 1,000 years later.

In 1506, an Italian architect named Donato Bramante began to reconstruct the church, or basilica, and planned to completely remove Constantine's edifice.

While constructing the new façade and court of the basilica, the workers discovered midway that they needed more stone. Their solution was to remove the elaborate marble facing from the abandoned Colosseum for use on the exterior of the basilica.

Work continued on the basilica for more than 100 years. Various artists, including Raphael, succeeded one another in the designing of the building. The definitive design was that of Michelangelo. Work was finally completed, and the new church was consecrated in November 1626.

The Basilica of St. Peter stands today as a monument to mentorship. All of the artisans, craftsmen and designers began their work knowing full well that *they would never see its completion in their lifetimes.*

Michelangelo and many others must have understood the need to teach succeeding generations the techniques and tools of their trade. The longer a great project or work takes, the longer it lasts, because more "investors" will carry it on through their ancestors.

The Colosseum has stood as a shameless monument of public disapproval for centuries. The furious way it was erected seemed to dedicate it to destruction; the use of slaves for its construction left no one endeared to its creation except its creators. Essentially, it was a sad monument to one man.

If you compare the lasting legacy of St. Peter's Basilica with the sad legacy of the Colosseum, you see how the combined investments of many selfless men and women in a labor of love far outweighed one despot's legacy of brutal vanity.

What can we learn from this ancient comparison? Include your family in planning your legacy. A young generation is left only to criticize your work if there is nothing left unfinished for them to complete themselves. All you have spent your life gathering and building can easily become a "rock quarry" from which they find and dismantle supplies for their dreams.

When our children are young, many of us feel it is more trouble than it's worth to ask for their help. However, there are hidden dividends when you include your children in small tasks while they are young. It is a great way to learn to work together.

Mentorship is easy when you tackle menial tasks together. A daughter has some of her deepest conversations with her mother while drying the dishes after dinner. Father and son learn to respect one another while working through the challenges of big and small repair and construction chores around the house and workshop.

This is a simple way to overcome the destructive cycle of "it's easier to do it myself." It also eliminates the childhood trap of a run-away-from-challenges mind-set. The same inclusion approach that built St. Peter's Basilica can help transform your home into a sanctuary. The best way to build a legacy that lasts is to lay a solid foundation of inclusion so that everyone has a sure footing on a future built together.

Notes
1. John 14:12.
2. John 17:22-23.
3. Philippians 4:9.
4. This theme is more fully developed in Tommy Tenney, *God's-Eye View* (Nashville, TN: Thomas Nelson Publishers, Inc., 2002).
5. Proverbs 4:7.
6. Joshua 5:9.
7. For a more detailed and expanded version of this principle, read *God's-Eye View*. This book focuses on the power of worship to provide divine perspective, transform our lives and plant hope in our hearts regardless of circumstances and obstacles in our way.
8. "Collapse: Why Do Civilizations Fall?—Mali and Songhai," *Annenberg/CPB*, http://www.learner.org/exhibits/collapse/mali.html (accessed December 31, 2001).
9. *Merriam-Webster's Collegiate Dictionary*, 10th ed., s.v. "Ming."

10. "Medieval Metal Masters." *Discover* (in association with The Gale Group and LookSmart), January 2000. http://www.findarticles.com/cf_0/m1511/1_21/58398776/p1/article.jhtml?term+Medieval+Metal+Masters (accessed December 31, 2001).

CHAPTER 6

RAISE UP A TEAM OF TORCHBEARERS!

Jesus told the church at Laodicea, "Because you are lukewarm, and neither cold nor hot, I will vomit you out of My mouth"![1]

Eli *assumed* Hannah was drunk and out of order because her passionate prayer was *different* or hotter than what he considered to be the norm. Are we enforcing some lukewarm or politically correct standard of worship today in our church services and meetings? God prefers blazing torches of praise and worship over subdued "cigarette lighter worship."

Eli was the high priest of Israel, so his chief assignment was to tend the flame of God and minister to Him. The Bible says Eli's sons did not know God and that revelation was rare in the days of Eli.[2] It seems Eli had nearly *snuffed out the flame of true worship* in Israel because he had failed to pass on to his sons the *heart relationship* of true priests toward God. These priests and spiritual leaders didn't even know God; they were in it for a paycheck and the job perks of the position.

The Lord was about to transform the barren spiritual landscape that dominated Israel during Eli's tenure as a keeper of the divine flame. He did it by answering the desperate prayer of a brokenhearted woman:

> Now Hannah spoke in her heart; only her lips moved, but her voice was not heard. Therefore *Eli thought* she was drunk. So Eli said to her, "How long will you be drunk? Put your wine away from you!" But Hannah answered and said, "No, my lord, I am a woman of sorrowful spirit. I have drunk neither wine nor intoxicating drink, but have *poured out my soul* before the LORD."[3]

This misunderstanding between the legalistic high priest and the desperate God chaser named Hannah was a prophetic act that accurately foreshadowed future events. God was out to replace flesh-dominated ritual with true spiritual worship.

Hannah the childless woman brought her brokenness to God in the disapproving shadow of Eli, the spiritually barren high priest. She desperately promised God *her seed* if He would give her a son. God heard her prayer and gave her the seed—Samuel—to sow back to Him in fulfillment of her promise. Then God planted Hannah's son as a seed to produce in a new future for Israel and His kingdom. (It wasn't the last time He would plant a Son to save future generations!)

HANNAH PROMISED GOD THE SEED OF HER PASSIONATE PRAYER

Well-meaning people with nearly extinguished passion may still misinterpret or try to snuff out the fire of passionate Hannahs in God's house today. They don't understand that He is actually *seeking* such passionate worshipers who will boldly worship Him in Spirit and in truth.[4]

God wants to raise up a *team* of torchbearers that will cross every line and overcome every obstacle dividing generation from generation or nation from nation.

Jesus came to make us *all* priests or designated keepers of the flame. Perhaps you've heard of the song in the book of Revelation that says:

> And they sang a new song, saying: "You are worthy to take the scroll, and to open its seals; for You were slain, and have redeemed us to God by Your blood out of every tribe and tongue and people and nation, and have *made us kings and priests to our God*; and we shall reign on the earth."[5]

TOMMY TENNEY

When my kids were little, we had a rare cold snap in Louisiana that dropped the temperature to an amazing nine degrees Fahrenheit. When ice coated the electrical lines in our unprepared southern territory, the entire region lost power. That meant the fireplace was the only source of heat in our house.

We decided to make the best of it and put our blankets on the floor near the fire. The problem was that since everybody else promptly went to sleep, I wouldn't be sleeping much. By default, I had received the assignment (and very unfamiliar task) of tending the fire that kept us warm during that dangerous ice storm.

I learned firsthand that night that it is far easier to start a fire than to keep it going. Every time I thought it was safe to nod off in fitful sleep, I had to get up again and roll another log on the fire. The role of flame tender would have been much easier if someone else would have joined me in the task that night.

GOD IS SERIOUS: HE WANTS US TO KEEP HIS LAMP BURNING

Young Samuel probably didn't realize that he was in the center of God's plan when he kissed his mother good-bye, but passion returned to God's house the day he began to serve with Eli the priest in the tabernacle of the Lord.

God is serious about preserving the flame of divine passion and intimacy in His presence. He will go to great lengths to provide for Himself a faithful flame keeper.

Now the boy Samuel ministered to the LORD before Eli. And the word of the LORD was rare in those days; there was no widespread revelation. And it came to pass at that time, while Eli was lying down in his place, and when his eyes had begun to *grow so dim that he could not see,* and *before the lamp of God went out in the tabernacle of the LORD* where the ark of God was, and while Samuel was lying down, that the LORD called Samuel. And he answered, "Here I am!"[6]

There is more to this story than meets the eye. It represents a leader's failure to impart passion for God to future generations. It also reveals just how far God will go to bring His plans to pass and correct problems created by human failure and disobedience.

God is just as interested in preserving His purposes *today* as He was in Samuel's day!

AMIE DOCKERY

One day during a holiday season, I was assigned the duty of keeping a fire going (just as Tommy was during the ice storm). All day long one question rang through the house, "Who let the fire go out?" (as if everyone didn't know).

I didn't willingly neglect the fire. I just walked out of the room to do something and forgot about it. And before I knew it someone would feel a draft and call for me to get it going again. It wasn't difficult to keep it hot when I was near. But I was continually being distracted by something else that I wanted to do and was lured away from the warmth of the fire and out of the room.

Distractions are dangerous when you are trying to keep the flames of a fire bright and hot. They become even more dangerous to second-generation flame tenders. We are referring to people who go to church out of duty or tradition as if they were volunteered for the job by virtue of their family relationship rather than by personal choice.

YOUR JOB IS TO MINISTER TO ME!

Serious problems arise when the children of flame tenders (or God chasers) get volunteered as God chasers by title before they fall in love with God themselves.

Children who grow up in a Christian home aren't automatically Christians. They must enter the Kingdom the same way everyone else does—they must repent of their sin, receive forgiveness through the blood of Jesus and receive Him as Lord and Savior.

AMIE DOCKERY

As a PK (preacher's kid), I often felt separated from other kids and their families because of the differences in our lifestyles. While other kids were going to Little League, gymnastics and summer camp, I was making memories at our church's work nights, food drives for the poor and doing volunteer work at benefit Christmas tree lots and fireworks stands. Some of the very best times of my life were spent at church-organized events.

I noticed that other families had special things or activities around which their lives revolved. In contrast, our family life always had an overriding element of seriousness in it. We laughed and had good times like everyone else, yet I was constantly aware of the mission set before us.

Everything we did had a purpose, because it was out of purpose that we had begun. Somehow in that process, I managed to capture the passion my mother and father felt for God and the ministry.

Now as a parent of four PKs, I have chosen to limit the distractions by carefully balancing their desires for involvement in extra activities with the necessary commitment to our church. We don't participate in activities that conflict with regular church services because I want my children to retain the conviction that God's kingdom must come first.

Eli's sons knew they would follow in their father's footsteps even as young boys. It was part of the family vocation and cultural tradition. Yet for some reason, they only became "pretend" priests who never truly ministered to God from the heart.

Samuel, on the other hand, was born literally because God responded to his mother's passionate prayer and sacrificial covenant with Him. Samuel received a spiritual inheritance that somehow escaped Eli's sons.

KEEPERS OF THE FLAME

God commanded Aaron and the Levite priests of the Old Testament to keep the fire on the altar in the Tabernacle going constantly.[7] In the Bible, fire often represents God's tangible presence and man's passionate response to Him. This was the flame that went out under the dim-sighted oversight of Eli.

In the Bible, fire often represents God's tangible presence and man's passionate response to Him.

Why did God choose fire to represent Himself at times? Perhaps because it seems to have an inner life of its own. Fire responds to the abundance of dry, or hungry, fuel, and it seems to thrive under the influence of winds and breezes. It also seems capable of disappearing when it is smothered, quenched or left unattended.

Why would God choose to represent His presence with something that required such diligent human maintenance? After all, He is God. He doesn't need our involvement, does He?

Could it be that God chose fire to represent the habitation of His presence among men because fire never remains long among us unless it is really wanted, appreciated and constantly fed?

Fire can come suddenly and without notice in the form of a forest fire or explosion of some kind. However, it won't remain long once the source that feeds it is gone. God's presence never abides long where He isn't wanted.

The primary duty of the ancient high priest was to tend the flame of God. It was his responsibility to provide all that was required to perpetually welcome and maintain God's presence among men.

The Bible says that in Eli's day, "the word of the LORD was precious . . . there was no open vision."[8] If Eli was going blind at the time young Samuel arrived, could it be that his blindness was a physical manifestation of the *spiritual blindness* he and his sons had brought upon Israel?

We must do whatever it takes to preserve our spiritual vision. Vision is a result of two factors: the ability to see and the presence of enough light to see. If either one is limited or lost, we may lose the ability to see with "open vision."

The first symptoms of blindness include a lack of perception and a dangerous blurring of the light. Apart from disease, you can lose vision in at least two ways. You can lose it when time steals your ability to see through the natural aging process, or you can lose vision by losing all available light to see by.

Imagine trying to drive a car at night with sunglasses. Now imagine doing the same without the sunglasses, but also without any headlights, street lamps or illumination from other vehicles. Either situation is dangerous, but if you combine both situations, your drive is probably destined for an abrupt end.

Sin brought dim spiritual perception to Eli and removed the light of prophetic illumination from his nation. It can do the same thing to us today.

PREVENT SPIRITUAL BLINDNESS: THE CANCER OF THE FUTURE

If vision is understood to be spiritual guidance, foresight or divine direction, then the loss of vision can prove deadly to destiny. Spiritual blindness is the cancer of the future; it robs purpose from future generations.

How do we preserve vision in our lives and in the Church?

First, we must prepare for the future by passing on to our children and their children a burning passion for God and His kingdom. Then they will see clearly long after we are gone from the scene. Second, we must make sure we keep the fire of God burning in our hearts and congregations so that the light of God's presence will stay bright.

TOMMY TENNEY

While I was working on this book with Amie at our ministry offices, her mother walked into our conference room with some coffee for her daughter and asked her something. Amie's mother and I come from the same generation (although she looks much younger), and when she came in the room and asked the question, I couldn't tell to whom she was talking.

I hate to admit it, but I actually had to put on my new trifocals to see if she was talking to me or to Amie. Age and time tend to blur the lines, and sometimes we don't know who is talking to whom. Perhaps this is why it took Eli three tries to work through his blurred perception of God's first conversation with young Samuel (who had never heard the Lord's voice before that night).[9]

We must raise up the next generation and help them discover, develop and release their abilities in Christ. If we do our job well, this newer and younger generation will march into God's purposes with fresh vision.

Fire has a profound effect upon those who are near it. It warms our bodies, comforts our souls and illuminates the surroundings of those in close proximity to its flames. In the same way, those who draw near to God's presence are warmed, comforted and given revelation by Him.

Just as fire will ignite nearly everything that draws close enough to its heat, so will the presence of God ignite passion in the heart of anyone who comes close enough to Him. People who draw near to God clearly understand their calling and divine destiny, but those who wander far from Him inevitably find themselves in the cold darkness of spiritual confusion.

STAY IN THE HEAT AND UNDER THE INFLUENCE

When you move away from the flames of a fire, the fire itself does not change but the effect and influence of its light and heat are diminished by distance. The same is true when you pull away from the presence of God. In addition, you may also become open to distraction.

AMIE DOCKERY

One day while watching a children's show with my kids, I saw a furry little blue creature run away from the camera as a nasal voice repeatedly said, "Far . . . far . . . far."

I laughed as the character bobbed backwards to the top corner of the television screen and swung his furry leg over a cardboard cutout of a mountain. Then he yelled at his viewers with a rich vibrato, "Far!"

Moments later, the same creature appeared so close to the television camera that the kids and I could barely make out the details of his furry face. This time he whispered, "Near." Perhaps we all need to consider this simple lesson on "near" and "far" and consider these words from God's Word:

> But it is good for me to draw *near* to God; I have put my trust in the LORD GOD, that I may declare all Your works.[10]

> These people draw *near* to Me with their mouth, and honor Me with their lips, but their heart is *far* from Me.[11]

Is it possible that Eli the high priest looked away from the flame of God long enough to be distracted and undermined by the sins of his sons, Hophni and Phinehas? They had wandered far away from the presence of God. In fact, Eli's sons were busy committing acts of fornication and adultery with women who served at the far end of the priestly compound at the entrance to the tent of meeting. This was as far from the flame in the holy place and the righteousness of God as these so-called priests could get.[12]

Meanwhile, Eli was losing his vision and the lamp of God was going out. Hannah's prayer was knocking at the door of destiny. Is your passion for God knocking on destiny's door?

Notes

1. Revelation 3:16.
2. According to 1 Samuel 3:1, revelation or intimate knowledge of God and His purposes was *rare* in Eli's day.
3. 1 Samuel 1:13-15, emphasis added.
4. See John 4:23.
5. Revelation 5:9-10, emphasis added.
6. 1 Samuel 3:1-4, emphasis added.
7. See Leviticus 6:12-13.
8. 1 Samuel 3:1, *KJV*.
9. See 1 Samuel 3:2-8.
10. Psalm 73:28, emphasis added.
11. Matthew 15:8, emphasis added.
12. See 1 Samuel 2:22—3:2.

CHAPTER 7

PREPARE
SOMETHING
TO LEAVE
(AND BE THERE TO RECEIVE)

The scene must have stunned onlookers thousands of years ago when Samuel "ministered before the LORD, *even as a child, wearing a linen ephod.*"[1]

The linen ephod was reserved solely for the priests who served in the holy place and behind the veil of separation. The impact of little Samuel's ministering to the Lord was even greater because, as long as most of the people could remember, old Eli had been the primary priest who ministered to the Lord.

As for the high priest's two sons, they supervised the animal sacrifices (while choosing the best portion of meat for themselves) and committed immoral acts with women at the front door of the Tabernacle.

The situation must have baffled the people who saw all of this going on. Who could help but wonder when young Samuel ministered to the Lord as if he were born to it, while Eli's grown sons ministered solely to their own sinful pleasures. One thing was certain—*little Samuel didn't get there by himself.*

His miracle began with his praying momma. Samuel's mother dedicated her son of promise to God *before* his conception and birth. Then she kept her promise and committed Samuel to Eli's care after she weaned him. This is a parent who positioned her son for divine purpose in two ways: She dedicated him to the Lord from the beginning, and she released him to someone else for specialized mentoring.

POSITIONED FOR POWER

Some parents remain the dominant source of mentoring throughout a child's life, but the Bible also provides many examples of faithful parents who released their children to other mentors who, in turn, passed along spiritual legacies to their disciples. Unfortunately, far too few biological parents in the Church manage to impart spiritual legacies to their own children.

The parents of Moses and Samuel were unable to train their own children due to outward circumstances and personal commitments. Nevertheless, they were careful to position their sons for training by others who were leading their respective nations at the time. Other parents, including Abraham, Isaac and Jacob, managed to pass along personally their own spiritual heritage to later generations, delivering a blessing to the whole world. The methods may differ, but each of these families successfully delivered a spiritual heritage to future generations.

This biblical generation-to-generation model isn't very common in the Church today, and God must be tired of having to reignite His purposes all over again in each generation. This tired scenario repeats itself over and over again, because successive generations allow the fire to go out or fail to pass on the flame to their children.

God wants us to successfully pass on the "baton" of His passion, presence and glory from our hearts to the hearts of our children. This is one of the most important ways we can go from glory to glory on Earth.

The modern relay race presents a beautiful picture of the process of generational transfer, and the point of transfer seems to be at the heart of the problem.

The typical relay team includes four runners, with the final runner designated as the anchor in the race. The first runner tries to dash ahead of his competitors to carve a solid lead early in the race. All of this effort is wasted unless he cleanly passes on the baton to the middle runner. The second and third runners must hold their positions safely and then finally pass the baton smoothly to the anchor runner. The anchor hopes to clinch the race with a final burst of speed at the end when he crosses the finish line with baton in hand.

The passing of the baton from mentor to the mentored involves both straining forward and reaching back in unity of purpose—we succeed or fail together.

It should be obvious that relay races are won and lost not only through the speed of the runners but also through the split-second moment of transfer, when one runner passes a baton to the next. You may be the fastest person on Earth, but you will lose the race of life if you fail to pass the baton to the next generation.

Relay runners pass the baton to one another in "the box," a specific area on the track marked by a white line at the beginning and another line at the end. Even before the baton carrier arrives, the relief runner starts running while carefully pacing himself so that the two meet somewhere in the area between the white lines.

Most relay teams designate their fastest sprinter as the anchor, where a burst of speed is most needed. However, even the fastest runner cannot make up for a poor position created by faulty baton transfers. This is an excellent picture of our job as parents, mentors and spiritual leaders.

Life resembles a movie more than a snapshot because it moves continuously from conception to birth, through childhood and adolescence to adulthood and death. As we go through the seasons of life, each of us will be both mentors and the mentored.

Early in life, you will spend much of your time receiving from others and then kicking for the finish line in a burst of speed. In another season, your chief focus may be to strain forward so you can hand off the baton of God-ward passion to the next generation.

The passing of the baton from father to son, from mother to daughter and from mentor to the mentored involves both straining forward and reaching back in unity of purpose. For better or for worse, we succeed or fail *together*.

Samuel was one of the greatest prophets in the Old Testament, but perhaps the saddest statement we can make about him is that *he had no successors*. He had witnessed with his own eyes the sorrow caused by Eli's failure to pass a legacy to his sons. Yet just one generation later, Israel's elders told old Samuel, "Look, you are old, and *your sons do not walk in your ways*. Now make us a king to judge us like all the nations."[2]

It is often difficult to mentor your own children, but God still requires it. Samuel failed to mentor his own sons just as Eli failed miserably with his two sons. In the end, both of these fathers paid a high price for their failures. At least Samuel played an important part in passing his baton of spiritual leadership to a young shepherd named David.

He Wants a God Chaser, Not a Man Pleaser

Sometimes we don't even know who will run the anchor position on our team of life. This was the case with Samuel. He was a prophet, but he had no clue as to who would rule Israel after Saul. Using his own discernment, Samuel the prophet chose an obvious leader with tremendous charisma, and God stopped him cold. *God was looking for a God chaser, not just another man pleaser.*[3]

God knows the name of the next runner, but most of us won't know who we're passing the baton to until we enter the box of transition. It could be our own children, it could be our descendants 200 years from now, or it may be an "adopted" son or daughter whom God sends into our lives for mentoring.

In God's view, we are a family or body with many members, and each member has unique abilities, strengths and qualities. He wants us to learn how to work together for His kingdom and make allowances for each of our individual sets of strengths and weaknesses.

Some of us run steady and unmoved in the face of discouragement, but others may easily become discouraged if placed in the first or second leg of the race. However, they may be great anchor runners, anointed to cross the finish line in a burst of speed. Each of us must find our proper place in the race.

Why are we spending so much time talking about passing a baton in a relay race? *Unsuccessful mentoring often trips future generations just at the crucial point of transfer, causing the baton to be dropped!*

One of the most devastating of these failed transitions in Bible history occurred during the reign of Judah's King Jehoiakim. God delivered a stern prophecy to Judah through Jeremiah, offering the people a chance to repent and protect their future. The people wanted to repent, but King Jehoiakim hardened his heart and cut apart the scroll on which the prophecy was written.

Jehoiakim burned the scrolls in front of his princes in open defiance of God and received one of the most frightening judgments in the Bible: "Therefore thus says the LORD concerning Jehoiakim king of Judah: 'He shall *have no one* to sit on the throne of David.'"[4]

God promptly had Jeremiah dictate another scroll, as if to say, "My purposes will go forward, even if I have to *cut you off.*" The prophecy came to pass, and Jehoiakim's throne was filled by someone from another bloodline rather than by the king's son.[5]

Most Christians know that God's first command to Adam was, "Be fruitful, and multiply, and replenish the earth."[6] We usually interpret this as a purely physical or natural command about having children (and it seems we have the physical part of this command covered).

Perhaps the *real* question is, Have we reproduced and multiplied the *"likeness of God"* in the world? Have we lifted future generations on our

TOMMY TENNEY

Nearly every Christmas season I preach a message about God's divine solution to the Jehoiakim problem. God promised David there would always be a son in his line reigning on the throne. Yet Jehoiakim, a descendant in David's royal bloodline, brought a curse on everyone in that family line. This divine conundrum, or puzzle, seemed to lock the door of destiny for David's seed. It demanded a divine key, the "key of David."[7]

Joseph, the espoused husband of Mary, was a direct descendant through Jehoiakim's cursed bloodline. Mary was also a *direct descendant of David,* but not of the royal line. According to the Law, any son delivered through Mary had a legitimate right to the throne of David because she was married to Joseph. Since Mary conceived of the Holy Ghost and not through Joseph, the blood of David flowed through Jesus' veins, with none of the cursed blood from Jehoiakim's line. God will fulfill His purposes even if we fail to pass the baton to the next generation (but it is *better* to do things God's way).

shoulders to capture the full measure of divine inspiration, impartation and passion for God's purposes?

When you lift your children to your shoulders or elevate those you mentor in the things of God, you are literally wearing your future on your shoulders.

SINGLED OUT TO LIFT HOLY THINGS TO THEIR SHOULDERS

God's purposes have always been carried on the shoulders of men. For example, God singled out the sons of Kohath from among the Levites and exempted them from routine tasks, so they could carry the holy implements of worship used in the Tabernacle. In fact, they were told to carry all holy things *on their shoulders!*[8]

Apparently, this knowledge was lost within one generation after the Philistines killed Eli's sons and captured the ark. Years later, David had to rediscover the importance of the dented shoulders of men to properly transport the ark of God's presence to Jerusalem.[9]

David danced for joy before the ark as the priests lifted *Israel's future* on their shoulders and carried it back to Jerusalem. In the same way, joy should overtake us when a godly parent picks up his young child and perches him on his shoulders, because he is literally lifting his future on his shoulders.

The same thing happens when we extend a helping hand to any member of the next generation. As mentors, we must hoist them up on the platform of our lives and faith in Christ. God commissions us to help them see the future from the shoulders of their spiritual fathers and mothers. We should share the confession of the mother who was asked if the child on her shoulders was getting heavy: "She ain't heavy—I'm her mother."

> *It is God's plan for us to lift and carry God's heritage—our physical and spiritual children—as sacred things on our dented shoulders.*

Under the New Covenant, we are *all* priests. It is God's plan for us to lift and carry God's heritage—our physical and spiritual children—as sacred things on our dented shoulders. As spiritual Levites, we have an obligation to train our children to tend the fire of God with the fuel of their hearts. This obligation applies whether you are a bread baker, preacher, accountant or bank president.

Who will teach us how to be parents? Ideally, we learn how to parent from our parents (and *their* parents). Unfortunately, it is common for the natural parenting chain to be broken in today's divorce-prone society. If that is your situation, you must trust God to lead you to other fathers and mothers in the Body of Christ who will take you in and "adopt" you as their own.

God wants each generation to pass to the next the best of its accumulated knowledge, experience, conviction and desire. Each of us is perched on a limb of the spiritual family tree, supported by the actions, experiences and accomplishments of those who went before us. This tree is not planted and nurtured by *genetic* connection but by *spiritual* impartation and instruction. For this reason, the neglect of a parent may forfeit an opportunity to sow into the next generation.

Since life consists of continuous cycles of seedtime and harvest, you are a seed whether you want to be or not. You have already made an impression on everyone who knows you, for better or for worse. People know and catch what you truly believe, not through some long doctrinal statement you have memorized, but through your public lifestyle and personal actions.

In other words, there is no way to falsify your spiritual DNA. You can only produce in others what you are. It has been rightly said over the years, "More is caught than taught."

Each of us has the opportunity and obligation to pass on a legacy to the next generation. But first we face the choice to receive the legacy we are given and add to it, or to reject it and essentially erase its effect on future generations.

What kind of power and influence would be released if the spiritual legacies of multiple generations combined together in one generation today?

AMIE DOCKERY

While working on this manuscript, I told the Lord that I could see some of the obstacles we face in passing on a spiritual legacy, but I wanted to see more than obstacles or problems. What good is a book if it only lists the problems without offering any proven solutions? I prayed for answers and I sensed Him say to me, "Prepare and be there."

That was a lesson in itself. God never gives an individual all of the answers. We need one another to complete the circle and please Him through unity. The completed message of this chapter and book is, *Prepare something to leave and be there to receive.*

All members of a mentored or future generation have the privilege and obligation to receive the legacies of those who mentor them in Christ. Yet their greatest attributes may easily become their greatest weaknesses in the process. They must beware of any desire to *control* that legacy or impose fleshly conditions on a spiritual calling.

The greatest obstacle to your destiny may come from *within* you rather than from some outward demonic attack or negative circumstance. Especially guard against pride. Make sure you don't ask God to bless your blind pursuit of cherished personal desires. Search His Word and seek His purposes *first* before you lay any plans or ask God to bless something you want to do.

Discover God's will and make it your own. A driving desire to take over the management of your life may tempt you to seize the reins of destiny from God's guiding hands. Don't believe the lie of the world and run after your own identity. You discover your identity by passionately pursuing the Prince of Peace.

AMIE DOCKERY

At one point in our marriage, my husband and I began to pray about moving with our two children to another state. We both worked at my parents' church and were fairly happy, but I felt that I would never be regarded as an adult if we didn't move away for a while. Yet I also knew in my spirit that leaving to live elsewhere was a second best solution.

Finally, a guest speaker confirmed the direction I felt in my heart when she said, "If you go, God will bless you, but that blessing cannot compare to the reward you will receive by staying and submitting. No one else can do what God has called you to do in this house. There is a direct inheritance in store for you here."

Many sons and daughters in the Bible were tempted to run from the plan of God. Success came to those who were tenacious enough to stay in a productive relationship with their parents or mentors.

Ruth had plenty of reasons to return to the safety and comfort of her old life after her husband died. She was childless and without an inheritance, so naturally she had no reason to stay with her mother-in-law. Nevertheless, Ruth remained and took on every detail of Naomi's biblical heritage as a descendant of Abraham. She vowed that Naomi's God would be her God, and her godly persistence produced a spiritual inheritance that still blesses us today.

God placed the power within us to combine the anointing, calling, wisdom and intimacy of the previous generation with our own, and then to pass on that spiritual wealth to the *next* generation! He intends to transform human destiny by joining together multiple generations to produce a powerful and lasting legacy of the Kingdom.

There is more to leaving and receiving a spiritual legacy than just being alive. Stop what you are doing and invest the time to lift your children and the next generation to your shoulders. Give them a glimpse of God's glory from the platform of your life experiences and wisdom in God's Word. Let them see a broad vision of their destiny and then help them get there. We have a holy mandate to *carry God's inheritance into the future.*

AMIE DOCKERY

My mother gave me a cherished possession that she received from my grandmother Molly Parker. It is an issue of *LIFE* magazine dated August 3, 1962. My grandmother was known to keep many old things, but this was a true treasure. Its worn pages preserve a priceless record of public opinion about two of the world's most famous and controversial people at that time: Marilyn Monroe and Oral Roberts.

The cover page of this issue of *LIFE* featured two dueling headlines: "Marilyn Monroe Pours Her Heart Out" and "Oral Roberts' Faith Healing Kingdom."

Marilyn Monroe's story was a classic Cinderella story of beauty and vulnerability marred by the complete absence of healing from childhood wounds that she so desperately needed.

Oral Roberts, on the other hand, was a young revivalist whose methods were greatly criticized by the media. He had dedicated his life to the restoration of others after being healed of an incurable disease as a young boy.

The articles are very different in nature and were not written to compare the two people, but the stark comparison between their lives is inescapable.

The article on Marilyn Monroe revolved around her position and accomplishments in the Hollywood film industry. She described the details of her rise to fame from obscurity and shared some of her feelings and failures. She was constantly aware of the public eye and she desperately desired to please her fans.

As I read her words, I began to understand just how deeply she examined the life she lived and the community she had committed herself to. She seemed to understand that she was living and giving to a universe *that only knew how to take.*

Marilyn said, "If you've noticed in Hollywood where millions and billions of dollars have been made, there aren't really any kind of monuments or museums. . . . Gee, nobody left anything behind; they grabbed it and they ran."

Oral Roberts's message on giving stood in obvious contrast to this, although his faith-based methods may have been mysterious to readers at the time. The *LIFE* article was written in a chiding and critical tone, but the virtue of Oral Roberts' message still rings true to this day.

The fruits of these two lives cannot be denied today. Although Marilyn Monroe is gone, lost in a tragic death, she is still celebrated in her Hollywood universe as one of its greatest sex symbols and most misused victims.

Dr. Oral Roberts managed to build Oral Roberts University in obedience to God's command. It stands today as a lasting testament *to a life lived to give.*

What a comparison—building your own universe or building your own university! Both stories graced one of the world's most prestigious magazines, and each had the trappings of public notoriety and fame in the beginning. Yet in our day, the monuments and accomplishments of only one of these people continues to live on and *give* to others while building the eternal kingdom of God.

Oral Roberts has continued for decades to father, mentor and empower men and women in person, through his teaching, his writing and Oral Roberts University. (Dr. Roberts graciously signed the cover of this historic issue of LIFE magazine for my parents on his 84th birthday, making it an even greater testament to a life lived to give.)

Magazine articles aside, whether you agree with Oral Roberts's theology is not the question. The question is whether you *want* to frustrate

God's purpose with your own version of "Marilyn's universe." Why not rejoice with those you mentored in your own "university"?

In the school of life there are no summer breaks. You are *always* teaching or learning (usually it is *both*)! The bell is ringing. Class is beginning. Somebody wants to perch on the shoulders of your knowledge and wisdom. Let your words and your life lift them up.

And while you mentor others, don't forget to thank those upon whose shoulders you sit!

Notes
1. 1 Samuel 2:18, emphasis added.
2. 1 Samuel 8:5, emphasis added.
3. See 1 Samuel 16:7, where the Lord warns Samuel to look, not at outward appearance, but at the heart.
4. Jeremiah 36:30, emphasis added.
5. See Jeremiah 37:1.
6. Genesis 1:28, *KJV*.
7. Revelation 3:7.
8. See Numbers 7:9.
9. See 2 Samuel 6; 1 Chronicles 15:2.

GOD*Chasers.network*

GodChasers.network is the ministry of Tommy and Jeannie Tenney. Their heart's desire is to see the presence and power of God fall—not just in churches, but on cities and communities all over the world.

How to contact us:

By Mail:

GodChasers.network
Post Office Box 3355
Pineville, Louisiana 71361
USA

By Phone:

Voice:	318.44CHASE (318.442.4273)
Fax:	318.442.6884
Orders:	888.433.3355

By Internet:

E-mail:	GodChaser@GodChasers.net
Website:	www.GodChasers.net

BOOKS BY

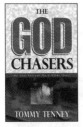

THE GOD CHASERS
$12.00 plus $4.50 S&H

What is a God Chaser? A person whose hunger exceeds his reach...a person whose passion for God's presence presses him to chase the impossible in hopes that the uncatchable might catch him.

The great GodChasers of the Scripture—Moses, Daniel, David—see how they were driven by hunger born of tasting His goodness. They had seen the invisible and nothing else satisfied. Add your name to the list. Come join the ranks of the God Chasers.

GOD'S EYE VIEW
$23.00 plus $4.50 S&H

In this simple but powerful book, worship will teach you "throne zone" secrets. The higher you go in worship, the bigger God appears (and the smaller your problems seem). If you can't see that from where you are presently sitting, there is a better seat available. The angels will usher you to your reserved seat in "heavenly places" and you will have *God's Eye View*.

CHASING GOD, SERVING MAN
$17.00 plus $4.50 S&H

Using the backdrop of Bethany and the house of Mary and Martha, Tommy Tenney biblically explores new territory. The revolutionary concepts in this book can change your life. You will discover who you really are (and unlock the secret of who "they" really are)!

PRAYERS OF A GODCHASER
$17.00 plus $4.50 S&H

In *Prayers of a GodChaser*, Tommy Tenney shares prayer—and principles of prayer—from the Bible that have revolutionized his life and his relationship to God. His passionate, heartfelt response to the prayers of Jesus, David, Hannah, and others will inspire and transform your prayer life. Let Tommy Tenney lead you into God's presence and you will learn to pray anew.

GodChasers.network
Post Office Box 3355, Pineville, Louisiana 71361-3355
318-44CHASE (318.442.4273)
www.GodChasers.net

Run With Us!

Become a GodChasers.network Monthly Revival Partner

G odChasers are people whose hunger for Him compels them to run—not walk—towards a deeper and more meaningful relationship with the Almighty! For them, it isn't just a casual pursuit. Traditional Sundays and Wednesdays aren't enough—they need Him everyday, in every situation and circumstance, the good times and bad. Are you a GodChaser? Do you believe the body of Christ needs Revival? If my mandate of personal, National and International Revival is a message that resonates in your spirit, I want you to prayfully consider Running with us! Our Revival Partners fuel GodChasers.network to bring the message of unity and the pursuit of His presence around the world! And the results are incredible, yet humbling. As a Revival Partner, your monthly seed becomes the matches we use to set Revival fires around the globe.

For your monthly support of at least thirty dollars or more, I will send you free, personal fuel each month. This could be audio or video-tapes of what I feel the Lord is saying that month. In addition, you will receive discounts on all of our ministry resources. Your Revival Partner status will automatically include you in invitation-only gatherings where I will minister in a more intimate setting.

I rely on our Revival Partners to intercede for the ministry in prayer and even minister with us at GodChaser gatherings around the country. I love to sow seed in peoples' lives and have learned that you can't out give God, He always multiplies the seed! If we give Him something to work with, there's no limit how many He can feed, or how many Revival fires can be started!

Will you run with us every month?

In Pursuit,

Tony Tenney

Tommy Tenney

Become a Monthly Revival Partner by calling or writing to:

Tommy Tenney/GodChasers.network
Post Office Box 3355
Pineville, Louisiana 71361-3355
318.44CHASE (318.442.4273)

Amie Dockery

In the balance of motherhood and
ministry I make time for occasions to
encourage others in the spiritual pursuit
of a more elevating life.

For speaking inquiries
or product information
please email your request to:
a.amied@verizon.net

Pictured above are my parents; Mike & Kathy
Hayes, my brother Stephen, my husband Stacey and
my four children Grayson, Stacen, Tate & Molly-Kate.

More Ways to Show and Share Love

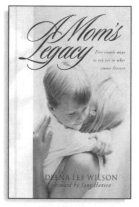

A Mom's Legacy
Five Simple Ways to Say Yes
to What Counts Forever
Deena Lee Wilson

Hardcover
ISBN 08307.23862

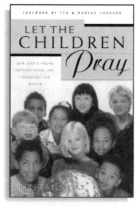

Let the Children Pray
How God's Young Intercessors
Are Changing the World
Esther Ilnisky

Paperback
ISBN 08307.25245

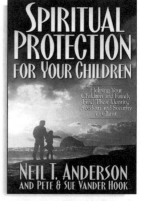

**Spiritual Protection for
Your Children**
Helping Your Children Find
Their Identity, Freedom
and Security in Christ
Neil T. Anderson and
Pete and *Sue Vander Hook*

Paperback
ISBN 08307.18869

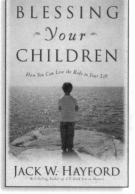

Blessing Your Children
How You Can Love the Kids
in Your Life
Jack W. Hayford

Paperback
ISBN 08307.30796

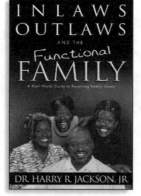

**In-Laws, Outlaws and the
Functional Family**
A Real-World Guide to
Resolving Family Issues
Dr. Harry R. Jackson, Jr.

Paperback
ISBN 08307.29674

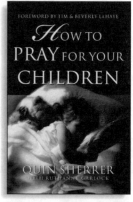

How to Pray for Your Children
Foreword by Tim and Beverly
LaHaye
Quin Sherrer and *Ruthanne
Garlock*

Paperback
ISBN 08307.22017

Available at your local Christian bookstore. www.regalbooks.com